arcocolourcollection

decoration

Residential Decoration

decoration

Author
Francisco Asensio Cerver

Publishing Director
Paco Asensio

Proofreading
Tobias Willett, José Serra

Graphic Design
Mireia Casanovas Soley

ISBN: 84-8185-015-2 (Complete collection)
84-8185-028-4 (Residential Decoration)

Residential Decoration

The intention of this study is to suggest themes, provide arguments and point out certain general tendencies which reflect the state of the contemporary residential decoration. This introduction seeks only to set forth some of the reasons which have given rise to the transformation of one of the social individual's natural demands (the house as a refuge) into something which sometimes comes dangerously near to the equivocal and ambiguous domain of art.

A summary of the factors influencing the evolution of domestic reality would be excessively long and fruitless. In the last few decades the concept of habitable space has undergone a series of mutations which are the logical consequence of the social changes in all aspects of life; the cultural, the economic, work and existential to name but a few. However, there is a tried and tested method of obtaining a knowledge of the heterogeneous and plural reality of residential interior design. It distinguishes between form and nature, sign and meaning, morphological and conceptual values.

All these factors have given rise to the fact the

home is no longer simply the stage for family life, since the very concept has evolved under the influence of new attitudes to life and living. Now, in contrast, the home has become the faithful reflection of the standard of living, not in the arrogant sense of decorative or extravagant luxury, but as a sense of individual affirmation built on sensations and experiences which materialise in different formal and technical solutions; the home has been transformed into a receiver of signs and information alien to its spiritual essence which frequently make it renounce its individual quality.

The technological revolution has pressuposed, on the other hand, the almost total triumph of science over the conventional needs and problems of domestic decoration. However, it has not been able to impose itself on the more conceptual aspects of the experience of domestic living. The theories of Le Corbusier have been able to triumph only in the area of function. Technology is applied as a means, not an end. Mankind does not seek absolute models of the home which are logical and rational, because this would represent a negation of the inherent essential values of the individual himself. Overall generalisation can only be applied in the practical field (distribution, organisation of use, technical solutions), leaving for decoration the more metaphysical dimension of the representation of a mental space.

The works displayed here are no more than a fragmented sample of the present state of residential decoration in which traditional figures alternate with certain lines of argument and technical traits which denote the effervescence of a creative field in which new and stimulating ways of resolving the problems of the domestic programme are constantly being investigated.

Residential Decoration

decoration

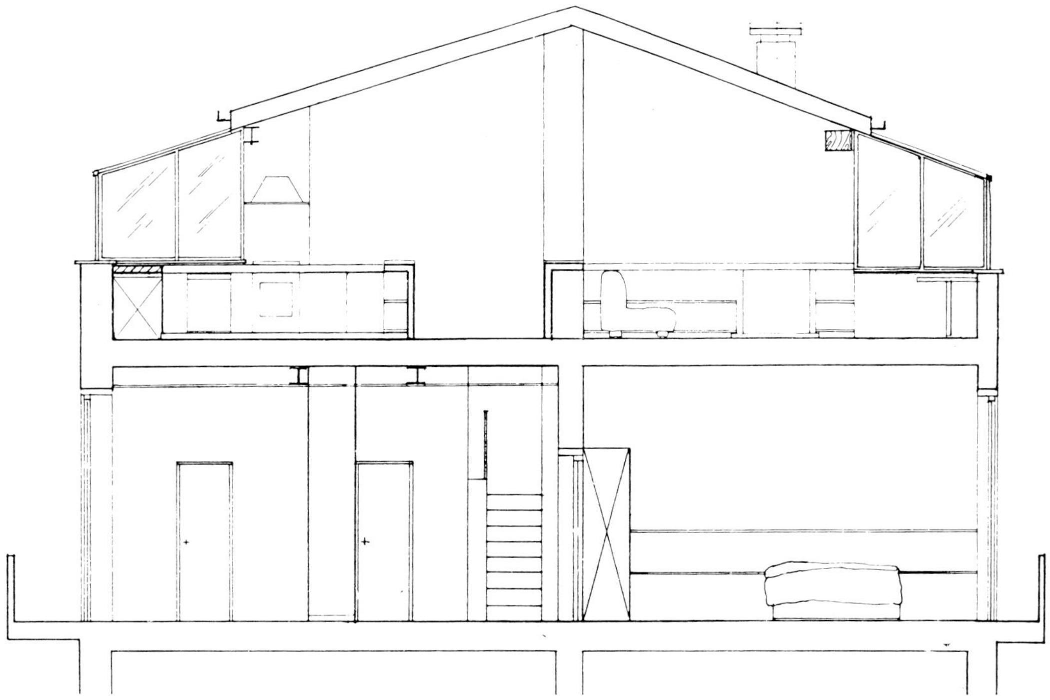

Cross section of both levels of the duplex.

Sottotetto a Milano

Carlo Santi

Born in 1925 in Milan, Carlo Santi is currently Professor of Urban Studies at the Faculty of Architecture of Milan Polytechnic. After receiving his degree, he worked in Givanni Muzio's studio. He has participated in several triennale and in the post-war round table on the urban development of Milan, coming out firmly against paving over the canals. In 1961 he received the Della Roca Foundation's National Town Planning Award. He spent 1965 conducting research at the Massachusetts Institute of Technology in Boston. He has worked for the Green Studio on the plan for the environmental and natural resources of the Milan territory, on the plan for the Roman historic centre of Milan, and on town planning projects for other cities. His professional projects in the field of architecture range from industrial facilities (the Pirelli head office in Verona, in collaboration with the architect Vittorio Borachia) to single-family houses. One of his chief concerns is small spaces, both residences (the Albavilla Casa Minima) and the interiors of cruise ships. His work is characterised by a marked interest in contrasts in the scale of architectural elements. His professional activities also included industrial design (for Arflex, Durlet and Zanotta) and the publication of several books, outstanding among them being L'uso dei modelli matematici nel campo degli studi urbani and Altro lavorare, altro abitare (1972).

The project considered here, undertaken by Carlo Santi consisted of the remodelling of a duplex in a tall, old building in Milan. The large windows of the attic offer vast panoramic views of the city. Although Milan is not *known for the beauty of its architecture, the sight is arresting, a true aerial cityscape of countless roofs, domes, church spires and neon signs.*

The apartment occupies the attic of the building and the floor immediately below it, and the distribution of its functional areas is symmetrical. The attic accommodates the day rooms, that is, the living room and the dining room, the kitchen, a bathroom and a pantry. An interior stairway descends from this level to the floor below, which contains two bedrooms, two bathrooms and a dressing room/closet. In addition, the duplex has two independent entrances from the main staircase that open onto each of the floors.

The most notable aspect of Carlo Santi's remodelling

The living area, decorated in light, cheerful tones, affords views across the rooftops.

The dining area, on the top floor; a French window leads to a secluded rooftop terrace.

Partial view of the living room, where natural light is used to full advantage.

project was the complete demolition of the partition walls between the rooms. The impression of spaciousness achieved through this technique is reinforced by the picture windows opened in the two wings, which allow the entrance of direct sunlight (none of the surrounding buildings are tall enough to block the light).

The result is an extremely luminous interior. Entering through the two opposite wings, the light tends to concentrate in the centre of the space. In order to regulate this powerful source of light, the architect installed a white screen with independent sliding panels in front of the athermanous glazing of the windows and the roof.

The distribution on the rectangular attic floor is symmetrical: the living room and dining room occupy the right half and the service rooms, the left. The door from the main stairway opens onto the service area where a small hall leads to the living room and dining room and to the kitchen and bathroom. The openings to the exterior are in the shortest sides of the rectangle, so that the rooms that enjoy the views of Milan are the living room and the kitchen.

The exposure of the beams, which were concealed by a suspended ceiling prior to the renovation, is another of the architectural accomplishments of the project. This was an ideal treatment for the pitched roof, and it recreated the timeless image of the attic as a romantic refuge.

But Carlo Santi went one step further; a thick, round beam (in reality, a rather straight tree trunk, supported with the aid of a larger beam perpendicular to the roof)

The diagonal timber dominates the space without constituting an obstacle in any way.

The rough finish to the beams provides an interesting contrast to that of the walls and ceiling.

Following Santi's removal of the partition walls, the arrangement of the upper floor is open-plan.

The comfortable, practical furnishings enhance luminosity and also serve to delimit different functional areas.

was positioned in the centre of the living room/dining room area, parallel to both the sloping roof and to one of the two couches in the living room, the couch with its back to the dining-room table. As a felled tree, this evocative presence of the world of nature also serves a distributing function, marking the limit between the dining-room and living-room areas. A bold addition on the part of the planner and a whim of the owners, who are fond of the sea, the roundness of the trunk recalls the mast of a sailboat.

In executing the internal two-flight stairway that links the floors, serena stone was used for the steps and metal tubing for the railing. All along the stairway, shelves at various levels, crowning a very thin partition built at the stairwell, interrupt the monotony of the whiteness. On their thin surfaces, also executed in the serena stone of the steps, stand wooden models of old ships, one of the enthusiasms of the young couple that live in the duplex.

The colour white is undoubtedly the most constant presence in the apartment. The walls are coated in plaster, the old beams that support the roof are painted gloss white, and the aluminium of the structures is varnished in the same colour. Even certain elements of the furnishings participate in this complicity to emphasise the interior light: the upholstery of the two living-room couches, the cabinets and the dining-room table are all white.

However, the neutrality of the whiteness does not make this belvedere/apartment bare and cold, as might be expected. On the contrary, because of the generous entrance of natural light that reflects the unusual tones of

the reddish wood of the parquet floor, at certain times of the day the whiteness is transformed into a warm rosy ambience.

Another colour whose strong presence is felt throughout the apartment is grey. With white in its composition, it is complementary to a certain extent. Pale grey serena stone was used for the steps of the interior stairway, the frame of the fireplace, the window stills, the surface of the dining-room table and other shelves and ledges, and its contribution to the decor is discrete and harmonious.

The above description might lead to an erroneous impression of this house as austere, containing the minimum of functional elements. A striking facet that

View from the living room window past the stairs to the kitchen.

The dominant white of the interior decoration is offset by unobtrusive, natural colours.

contradicts this notion is the lavish flooring of the living room, executed in French parquet with red Doussiè wood. Furthermore, the materials employed throughout and the decorative finishes create an environment in which comfort, although not necessarily the middle-class concept of comfort, plays the leading role.

The two white couches placed at right angles face a large wool carpet with geometric motifs in warm colours that contrast chromatically with the parquet. Other touches of color are provided by the red cushions of the couches, by the plants found everywhere in vases and hanging from the beam, and by the abstract geometrical painting above the fireplace.

The fireplace dominating the living room is completely lined in fireproof brick and is set into the above-mentioned frame of serena stone. The same stone is used for the paved area inserted in the parquet flooring just in front of the hearth to protect the wood from the burning coals of the fire. On the mantelpiece more models of old ships add a personal touch to this area. The fireplace is not really a practical necessity, but rather arises from the desire to create a romantic, environment, with reminiscences of a happier past.

The kitchen has an L-shaped work surface and an separate table for breakfast. Both the angular square surface and that of the work counter are of masonry, finished with small white tiles of acid-proof stoneware. The furniture built into this room was designed by the Bulthaup company. The kitchen sink has two basins positioned at an angle, efficiently handling the 90° angle,

View from the dining area to the stairwell and the kitchen beyond.

The practical yet aesthetic kitchen also commands a panoramic view.

while beside the cooker is a thick wooden board with vertical slits and a holder for knives and other cooking implements. Suspended by a wire over the table, an American aluminium lamp provides the artificial lighting for the kitchen. The most outstanding aspect of this section of the apartment is not so much the well thought-out arrangement of the partitions, but rather the splendid views of the Lombard capital and the sky, since the windows in the kitchen are extended to the roof.

A definitive evaluation of the project by this Italian architect involves a reflection on comfort, a concept that is naturally open to subjective interpretations. With this principle as his point of departure, Carlo Santi tends toward a type of interior design that, without rejecting a more stereotypical notion of beauty, has as its main objective the fulfillment of the specific needs of his clients, adapting his language to their tastes, personalities and lifestyles. This approach has little in common with the concept of the machine/house propounded by Le Corbusier. Although the latter reflects an attempt at universal application, the satisfaction of personal concrete needs is not considered, and for that reason its application was not successful in creating individual settings.

This Milan duplex offers an excellent example of the use of light as the structural material of the ambience, a perfect combination of the recreation of the romantic concept of the attic (the exposed beams, the fireplace) and a modern concept of comfort (the practicality of the kitchen, the warmth of the atmosphere).

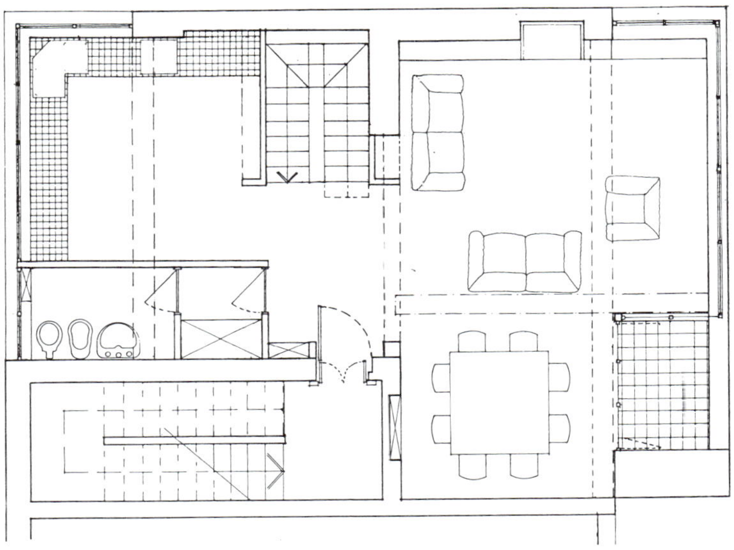

Ample natural light pours in through the windows-cum-skylights.

Plan of the upper floor.

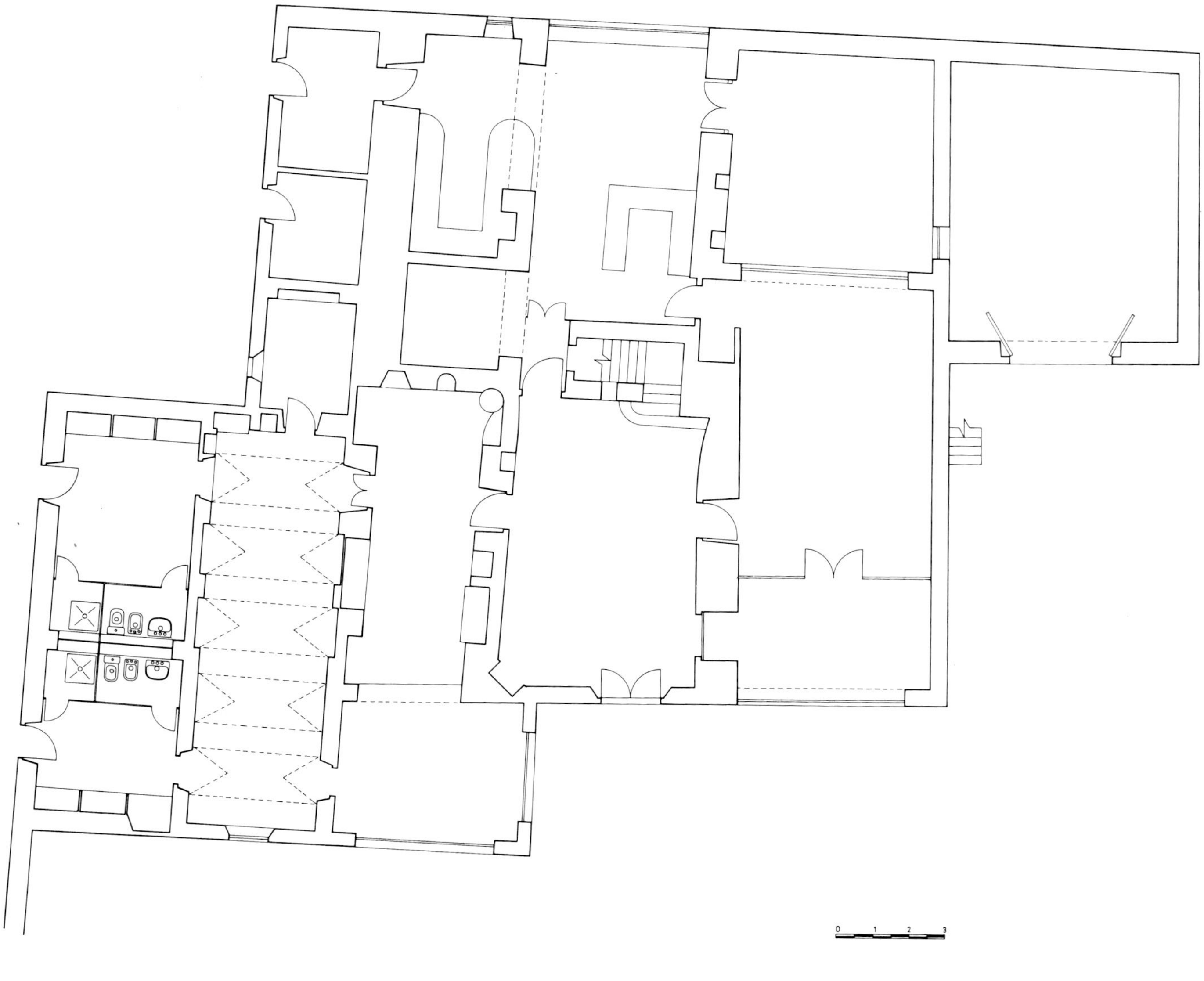
0
1
2
3

Floor plans of one of the different levels.

Tradition & modernity

BDM Arquitectos

Masía *is the generic name given to the rural dwellings in Catalonia, Spain. With local variations, it usually has the form of a basilica, with the south-facing main facade designed to shield the house against the prevailing winds.* Masías *can be small simple constructions belonging to tenant farmers and small proprietors; however, the term also includes the larger, more palatial constructions called* casas pairales, *which are sometimes veritable castles. The house remodelled by these architects belongs to the second category.*

The Empordà, where this building is located, is a plain situated inland from the Costa Brava, in the province of Girona, Spain. It had always been a wealthy region, even before the advent of tourism and it has a long cultural history going all the way back to Greek civilization. The marked Mediterranean flavour of the culture, landscape and architecture of the Empordà region has attracted a fair number of people distinguished in Catalan cultural, economic and political life, who have established their second residences in the area.

This renovation project, carried out between 1988 and 1990, was undertaken by three experienced architects from Barcelona: Manuel Briones, Tito Dalmau and Lorenzo Marqués, of BDM Arquitectos. Manuel Briones, who graduated in 1973, has taught in the Escuela de Arquitectura in Barcelona. His partner, Tito Dalmau, is likewise an architect, but also brings to this company his recognised talent in ceramic design, a field in which he has won various prizes. Lorenzo Marqués contributes his extensive professional experience in the world of

The lustrous floor sets off the elegant arched ceiling in the living room.

Perspective of the dining room, which opens onto an interior patio through the glass archway.

Floor plan of one of the levels.

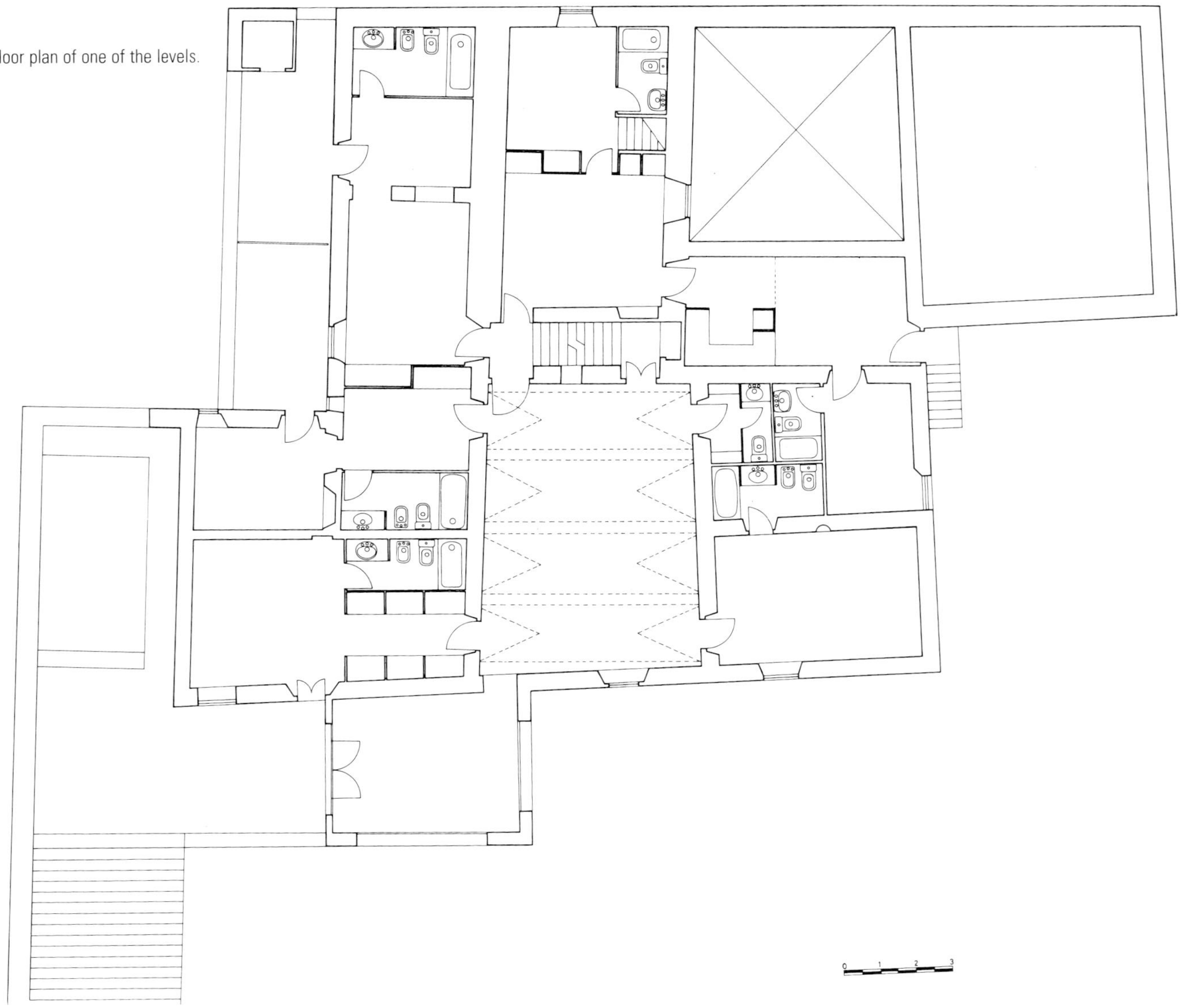

architecture to the group. BDM Arquitectos has also worked in interior decoration and design for private companies and government agencies. The work of these three professionals was recognized in 1981, when they were chosen as finalists for the FAD prize in architecture in Barcelona.

The location of the building was the first problem BDM had to deal with, since the house is situated at the bottom of a valley, and enjoyed a view from only one side, which was not the main facade. The aim of the remodelling project was to improve this unfavourable orientation in the medium term by employing two tactics. First an enclosed space next to the house was defined by the construction of several elements: the large entrance patio, a wall, the terraces and stone arches and a pergola. All of these elements have an undeniable aesthetic function, but they also define the appearance of the masía *more clearly within its setting. Secondly, emphasis was placed on the landscaping of the whole property, separating it and differentiating it from the surrounding emptiness. A series of elements form a barrier which excludes the less pleasant views: the vines which, seen from afar, draw the eye towards the house, making it look bigger; the olive trees which shelter it; the kitchen gardens; the palm trees and the semicircular swimming pool (protected from the wind by the enclosure wall). This natural barrier cuts the house off from the mountain and forest, the pinewood and the hedges.*

From the point of view of its construction, however, this masía *is a particularly attractive example of the local*

architecture. The unusual breadth of the centrelines and its almost perfect basilica form are both remarkable, as are the elegant vaulted ceiling of the main living room, and the small watchtower. The barrel vault ceiling on the ground floor was constructed using a method typical of the Empordà region using a concrete form made from reeds, which gives it an attractive texture.

The appearance of the outside of the building was restored and great care was taken to match the original finish so that the renovation would not be obvious. In particular, special care was taken to disguise work done on the stone walls and to produce a finish as similar as possible to that of the old walls.

BDM Arquitectos retained the preexisting structural

The exposed beams have been retained in most of the rooms. View of the master bedroom.

In some rooms, small spotlights on the wall directed towards the ceiling produce an attractive combination of natural and artificial light.

An elegant bathroom with designer accessories and dark parquet flooring.

divisions, limiting their intervention to assigning a function to each room according to the owner's requirements. Interior circulation has been somewhat modified; a few new doorways have been built in the same style as those already existing. Some windows have been shifted to make them coincide with the axis of the arches or alignments, which gives a more harmonious and coherent appearance to the entire house, a result of the skilful combination of its elements.

On the ground floor, in order to increase the amount of light entering the house and make the interior habitable, the end walls closing off the vaulted area, typical of the architecture of this region, were removed, opening the room to the exterior. With this modification the designers were able to create a sensation of spaciousness. The new walls enclosing these vaults and arches are made of glass set into the stone. The windows and doors, however, replicate the traditional design: the porticoed windows with wooden frames, and the wooden door framed with stone edging.

The final result of all these modifications is extremely effective. The effect is accentuated by the contrast between the rather unconventional and somewhat spectacular methods and textures used: the flooring, materials, wall and ceiling colours, lighting and a few

touches of modern design, such as the semi-reflecting glass panels which separate the bathroom cubicle from the master bedroom. This is complemented by the unusual furnishing of the house, based on furniture and accessories collected by the owners during their many trips abroad. Simplicity is the keynote of the decoration, giving rise to clean and elegant lines in the layout of the interior space. The bedrooms are decorated in light shades, as with the other furnishings – sofas, counterpanes, pillows and rugs. In some of the rooms, slender palms and other house plants enhance the cheerful feeling of rustic simplicity.

Vaulted ceilings and arches occur on all three floors, accentuating the height of the ceilings and the elegant and

The arches and vaulted ceilings occur repeatedly throughout the house and the high ceilings lend it an elegant and aristocratic air.

The decoration combines quiet discretion with elegance and a modern look.

aristocratic appearance of the rooms. The choice of a pale colour scheme on the high walls produces spacious and luminous interiors. Some parts of the internal walls, stairs and arches are stone, harmonising with the exterior walls of the building. The exposed beams have been retained in most of the rooms, giving the interior of the masía a rustic air. The floors are mainly dark polished parquet, illuminated by occasional spotlights as well as natural light. The bedroom floors have been covered with rugs and rush matting to achieve a warm, cosy atmosphere.

The decoration combines quiet discretion with elegance and modernity. The lighting is a key element; some of the rooms have large picture windows which look out over the property, while in others, where the windows are smaller, the designers have achieved a beautiful combination of natural and artificial light using spotlights which highlight the ceiling.

As a result of the renovation carried out by BDM Arquitectos this masía is poised on the borderline between the traditional and the modern, characterised by a cosy yet functional atmosphere. This contrast is an excellent design solution for this splendid example of rural Catalan architecture.

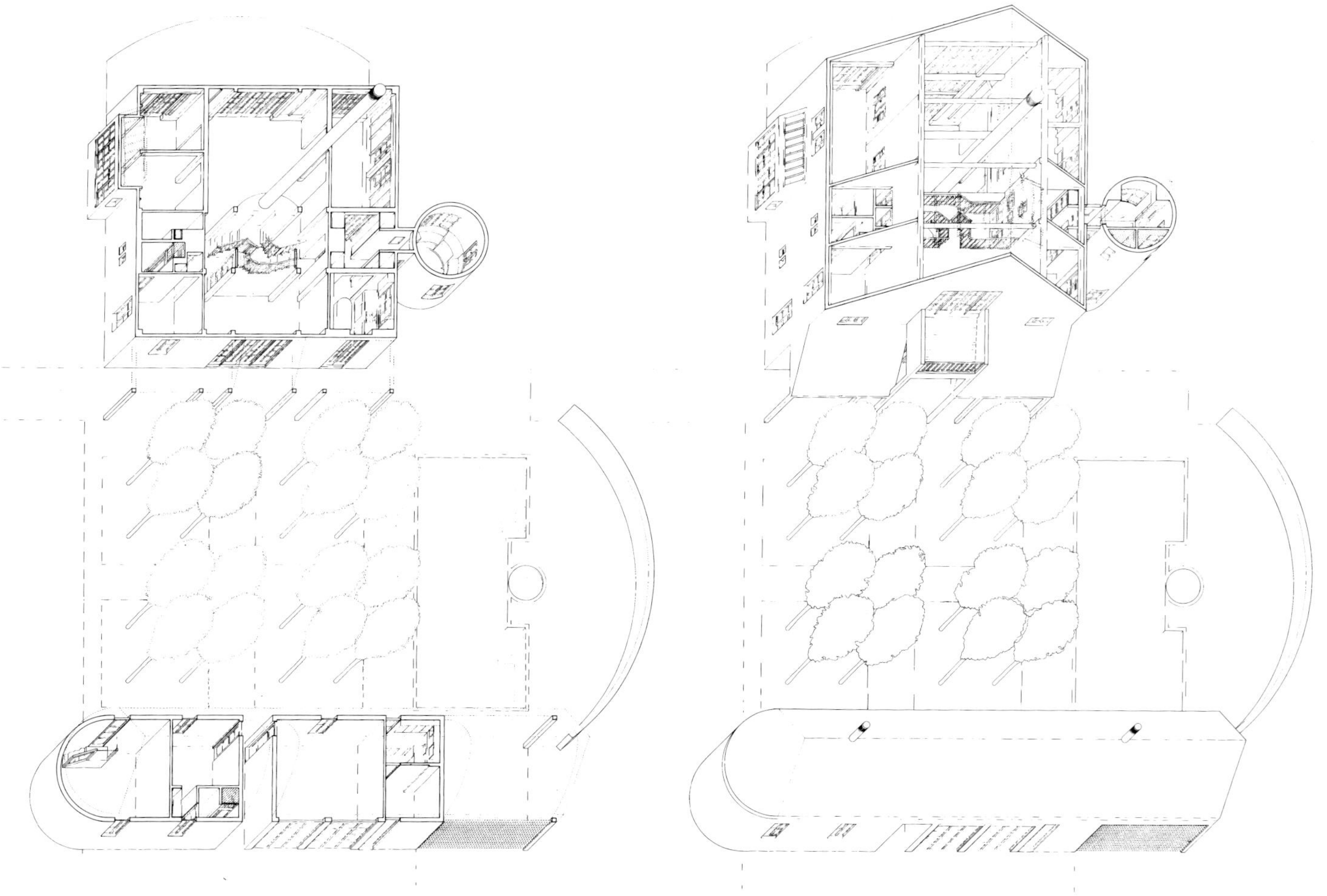

Axonometric views of the property.

In the purest country style

Charles Gwathmey & Robert Siegel

Spielberg House is the result of remodelling an XVIII*-century stable previously used as a barn. The structural shell, the external walls and the roof of the building have all been retained. It is located in the middle of quiet countryside, far from any towns, with beautiful views on all sides. Beside the house, to the northwest, there is a small lake which adds the final touch to this pastoral setting.*

The project was carried out by Gwathmey and Siegel. Charles Gwathmey was born in North Carolina in 1938. He studied Architecture at the University of Pennsylvania and received his Master's Dregree in Architecture from Yale University in 1962. Over the last twenty years, he has held faculty positions in the Schools of Architecture of several universities including Princeton, Texas, UCLA and North Carolina, and has been Visiting Professor at both Yale University and the Harvard Graduate School of Design. He was the youngest architect ever to receive the Arnold W. Brunner Prize from the American Academy Institute of Arts and Letters, and the only architect named by Time *magazine in their "Leadership in America" issue in 1974. In 1978, he became trustee of the Institute of Architecture and Urban Studies, and was subsequently elected President of the Board of Trustees. He has received various prizes throughout his career, including the Yale Alumni Arts Award in 1985 and the Guild Hall East Hampton Gold Medal for Visual Arts in 1989. He is currently a member of the President's Board of Advisors to the Yale School of Architecture.*

Born in New York in 1939, Robert Siegel graduated as an architect from the Pratt Institute in 1962. Upon

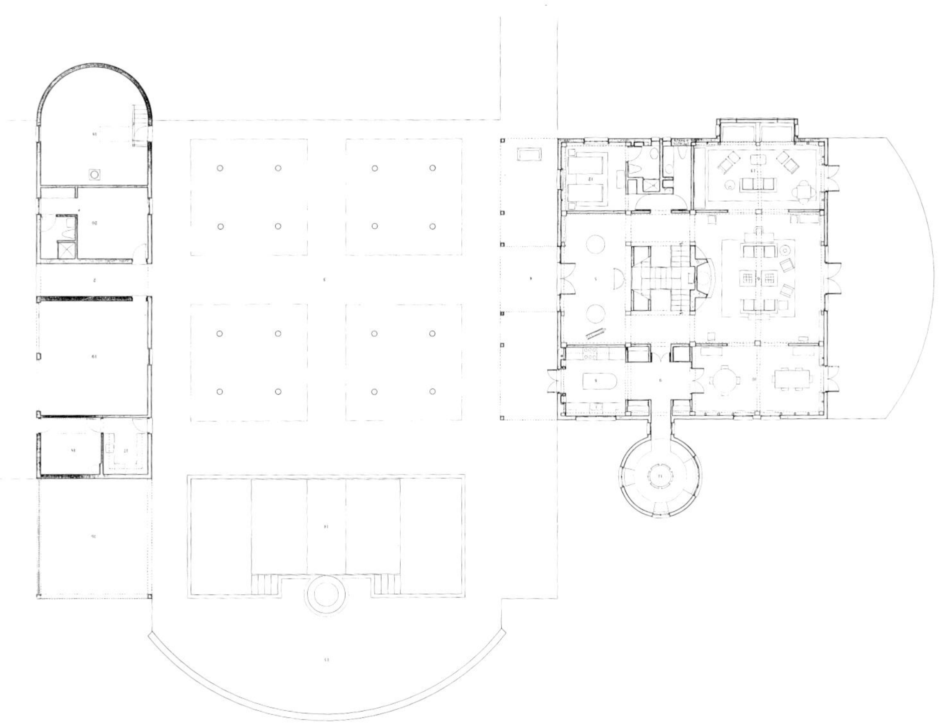

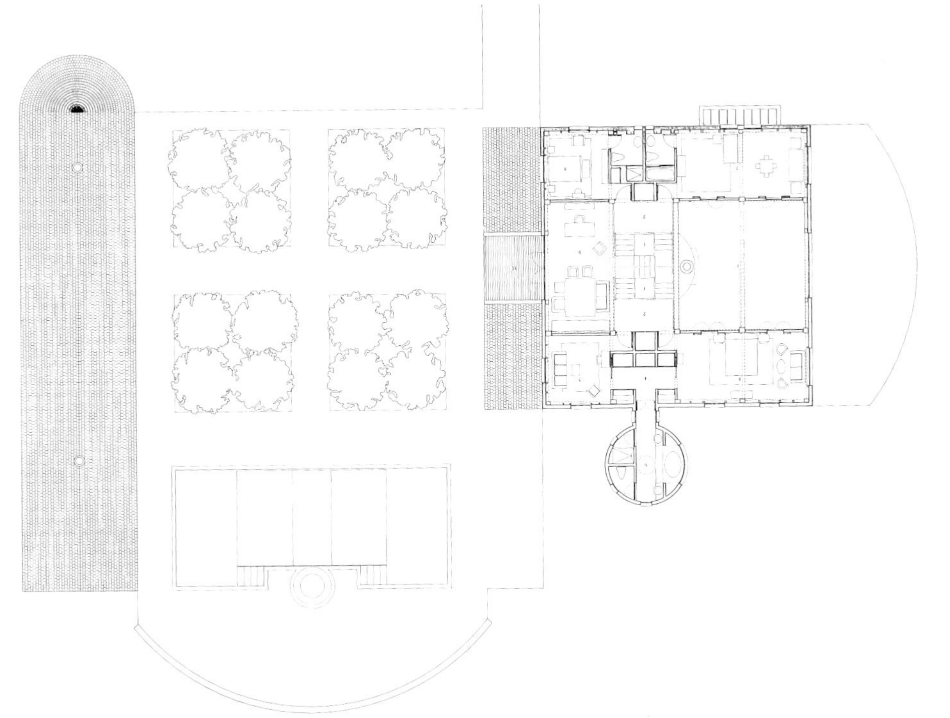

Floor plans of the different levels.

View past the foot of the stairs, with the living-room window in the background.

graduation he received the American Institute of Architects New York Chapter Student Award Gold Medal for design excellence. He continued his studies at Harvard University Graduate School of Design, where he obtained his Master's Degree in Architecture in 1963. He has held various positions including Vice President of the New York chapter of the AIA, Chairman of the Pratt Institute Board of Visitors and President of the Institute itself. In 1983 he set up the Pratt Institute Student Intern Program within the Gwathmey Siegel office. Five years later he and Gwathmey were jointly nominated for the International Design Magazine Hall of Fame, and in 1990 the New York Society of Architects honoured them with the Life Time Achievement Award in Architecture.

This project was built in East Hampton, New York, on a large site delimited to the northwest by a small lake. A long path lined with trees leads up to the residence and separates it from the road. The property is basically a rectangle occupied by a spacious courtyard, the "gate house" and the house Itself. There are a number of fruit trees planted in four clusters, separated by two paths in the form of a cross. This cross axis acts as a visual link between the lake and the driveway leading up to the house.

The long, narrow building has a porch, utility room and garage. This building is built at right angles to the

The lounge features a large fireplace which heats the room and creates a warm, cosy atmosphere.

The original supporting beams running from one side of the living room to the other have been retained.

house and serves as a "gate house", at the same time enclosing the property.

The house is divided into two floors which accommodate the traditional layout and rooms of a conventional home. On the ground floor, areas such as the entrance porch and the reception area have been joined together in order to increase the apparent size of the volumes. Comfort based on spaciousness determined the layout of this floor which has two living rooms, one smaller than the other. The upper floor houses all the bedrooms, each with en suite *bathroom and closely linked together.*

The larger sitting room has a double-height ceiling which enhances the sense of spaciousness. This room is where most of the family life takes place. It has a large fireplace, providing heat and creating a warm, cosy atmosphere. At one end – on the rear facade – this room opens onto the terrace, with a view of the pond in the distance. This whole external wall is composed of rows of windows, to let as much sunlight into the room as possible. The two lateral walls of this room have smaller windows. These, like the cross beams running from one side of the room to the other, were retained from the original structure. These rough wooden beams, which interrupt the void created by the removal of the upper floor, accentuate the rustic appearance of the house.

The smaller living room beside the large one is a continuation of the social and common living area. The two rooms are separated only by an old, thick wooden post. This room also provides direct access to the terrace, and on the opposite side, has a completely

TALKING
PICTURES

The double-height living room emphasises the interior spaciousness.

Interior of the kitchen.

A white stucco finish was used on nearly all the walls, including the bookshelves, the bathrooms and toilets.

glassed-in gallery connecting the interior to the garden. The spaces in this part of the house have also been made to look larger by the repeated use of glass doors and windows. The dining room, which is also closely connected and very sunny, is just beside the large living room, at the opposite end from the smaller sitting room.

The most striking feature of this house is the staircase connecting the two floors. It is a double flight entirely made of wood, located between the reception area and the living room. This complex structure connects with every level of the house on both sides, and even includes a mock flight of stairs which leads nowhere. The enormous staircase is lit from above by a skylight in the roof of the house. The sun shining in this window spreads an agreeable, warm light, accentuated by the shades of cinnamon, ochre, reds and browns of the interior colour scheme.

On the northern facade, there is a cylindrical structure attached to the building, which can be reached by a short passage. This structure is also divided into two floors; the lower one houses a breakfast room, and the upper contains the master bathroom. The original external structure of this building, previously the granary of the old house, has been conserved.

The renovation is evident in the master bedroom since the head of the bed clearly reveals the form of a fireplace bricked up by Gwathmey and Siegel. The sharp slope of the ceiling in this part of the house does not significantly reduce the space owing to the height of the room.

The floors throughout the house are covered with oak parquet, and the ceiling with oak veneer. Almost all the

original beams and columns have been retained. The woodwork on the doors and windows has all been painted a dark greyish-blue. The windows and exterior doors in the dining and living rooms can be closed with sliding wood panels. The fireplace in the main living room is whitewashed brick, as is the slim chimney that rises up from it to the roof. A white stucco finish was used on nearly all the walls including the bookshelves, the bathrooms and toilets.

This house retains the flavour of a traditional country house, in form as well as external appearance, re-creating the typical American country style and adapting it to contemporary needs. Inside, the decoration preserves a rustic atmosphere without being rough. The austere traditional furniture, clearly reminiscent of the country, is strategically arranged in a pleasant, quiet atmosphere. The architects have preserved the existing structural frame, exterior walls and roof and these elements serve as both a perceptual and psychological counterpoint to the new project. The resulting "graphic" is both compelling and pure.

The staircase connects with every level of the house on both sides, and even includes a mock flight of stairs which leads nowhere.

The symmetrical staircase forms the visual backbone of the house.

In the bedroom the headboard of the bed is a remodelled fireplace bricked up as a result of this renovation by Gwathmey and Siegel.

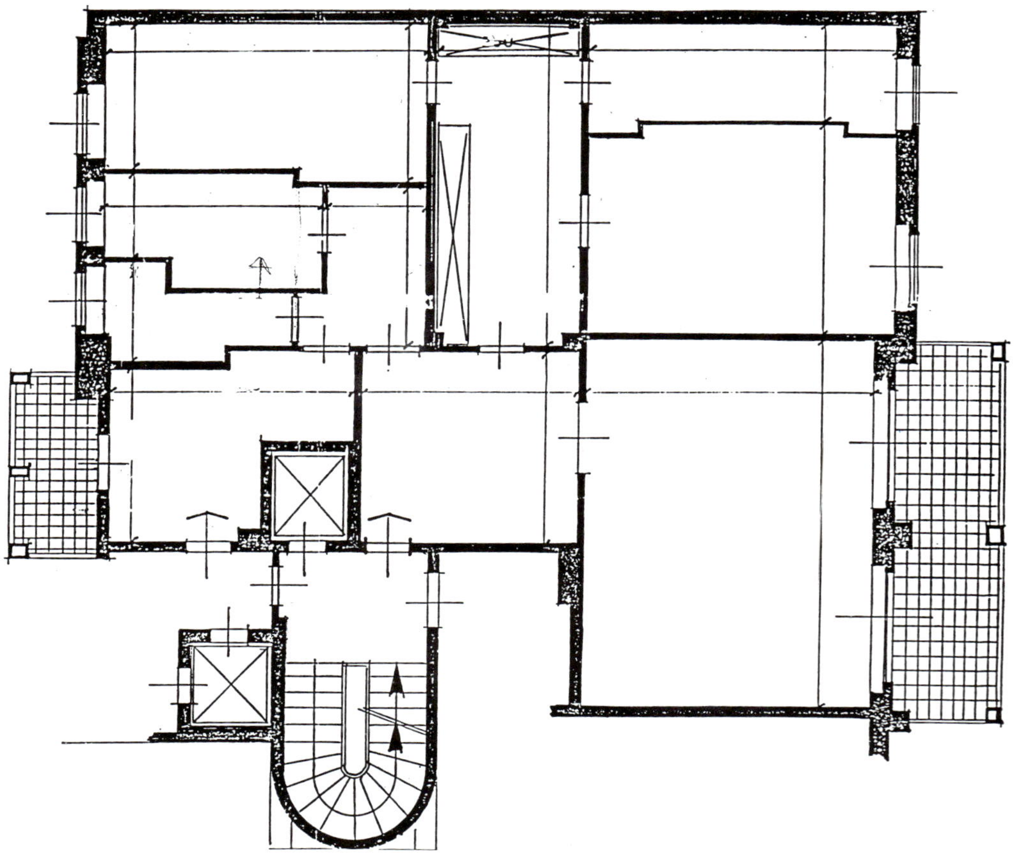

Sketch showing Raggi's design.

Floor plan of the former layout of the apartment.

Bonatti House

Franco Raggi

Born in Milan in 1945, Franco Raggi graduated in Architecture from Milan Polytechnic in 1969. From 1971 to 1975 he served as an editor on the magazine Casabella, *and later as editor-in-chief (1977-1980) and manager (1980-1983) of the design magazine* MODO. *In 1973 he was one of the organizers of the International Architecture Section of the Milan* Triennale *and the first critics' exhibition of revolutionary Italian design in the Berlin Internationale Design Zentrum. From 1975 to 1977 he acted as secretary/coordinator of the Visual Arts Section (Architecture) of the Venice Biennale and was the independent organiser of the exhibition* Europa America: architecture urbane-alternative suburbane. *In 1979 and 1980 he was in charge of the* Raccolta del Design *in the Milan* Triennale, *organising the exhibitions* Censimento del design *and* La casa decorata. *He organized more events of this type for the 1981 Biennale and the* Triennale *in 1983 and 1985. Since 1977, as an architect/planner, he has participated in numerous exhibitions (Bologne, Düsseldorf, Milan, Genoa, Toronto, Paris, Amsterdam, Tokyo and Basel), as well as in lectures and seminars. In 1985 and 1986 he taught at the University of Pescara's Faculty of Architecture and in 1989 at the European Institute of Design in Milan. In the course of his career he has produced architecture, interior design, books, magazines, stage sets and products. Outstanding among the latter are his designs for Fontana Arte, Cappellini, Poltronova, Luceplan, Tendentse, Roset Francia, Vetrerie Vistosi, Vetrerie Moretti and Kartell. In 1984 he collaborated on the new*

Floor plan of Raggi's design.

The wall of the living room forms a functional and aesthetic whole.

The sliding door in the living-room wall opens to reveal the study.

View from the entrance hall into the newly created dining room.

Detail of the built-in American cedarwood shelving in the study.

image of the Morassutti chain of retail shops. From 1984 to 1989 he advised Italtel Telematica on the design and development of its new products, and in 1986 he served as consultant for the image and household products of the company CROFF/Rinascente. In 1984 he conducted research for Fiat Auto on the evolution of signs and forms for electronic components in automobile design.

The remodelling of this apartment by Franco Raggi is proof of his loyalty to certain creative premises that stem from his obvious passion for both architecture and history. This passion permeates and underlies the genesis of each of the gestures, fragments and approaches in his work. In the field of residential interior design, he propounds a close relationship between decor, distribution and architecture. Raggi's intervention was not limited to a simple restructuring; rather, it served as a point of departure for the establishment of new laws regarding the layout of the residence. To this generating principle he has added the utilisation of historical, simulated and fictitious motifs, which evoke a previous existence, unreal and therefore fascinating.

All of the characteristics noted above are found in this new and lucid project. The apartment in question is located on the sixth floor of a building typical of upper-middle-class residential architecture of the fifties and sixties. The nature of the spatial distribution, therefore, reflected the conventional premises of that type of organisation, based on the conventional separation of service areas from living space. The existing layout and the uneconomical use of space was highly unsuited to

Raggi's references to the history of architecture and interior design resurface in this moulding.

Detail of the plaster relief with classical overtones in the entrance hall.

the requirements of the new owner, Maria Bonatti. The design was originally articulated around a blind central space that served as a mere point of transition to the rest of the rooms. Its only functional feature was several built-in closets.

In the context of this substandard distribution, Raggi's plan was based on two criteria: firstly, the architect's personality would not dominate the final result and, as a consequence, the needs of the client would take precedence in the planning process. The combination of these two principles resulted in a creative anonymity, an intervention in which the decorative elements introduced by the architect were not distinctive and inseparable signs of his own personality, but rather were chosen in an attempt to devise environmental referents attuned to the spirit and the needs of the owner.

In this case, Bonatti expressed her desire to make use of the space wasted in the original layout by turning it into a dining room (absent from the first programme), which would simultaneously act as a link between the rest of the rooms. She also proposed the definition of a work space, a study reserved for books and papers. With these basic objectives, the Milanese architect considered the possibilities offered by an interesting shell with a distribution typical of the sixties, and rather inadequate for present-day lifestyles.

The completed work was not simply the result of a modernization process. It also reflected a cultural and psychological interpretation of the wishes of his client. In this sense his architecture is that of a humanist who

View from the dining room into the hall, with its curved screen bearing the simulated Ionic column.

utilises his specialized talents for the benefit of the owner, avoiding the kitsch and the banal techniques in fashion until quite recently. Raggi's new concepts reflect a craftsman-like approach to industrial production, with special attention given to materials and detail, as well as a gradual interrelating of the fields of architecture, interior design, decor and furniture.

The purpose of the restructuring process was to make a more economical use of space than existed in the original, inferior layout, and to adapt the space obtained to a contemporary domestic programme. Thus, the central section that divided the services area from the living area was turned into a dining room. It was not closed off and isolated from the other rooms, but formed an ideal visual and physical link with the rest of the

The dining room and study are connected visually by two high openings.

Detail of the cedarwood doors with their carved directional arrows.

residence. In this sense it is not a room but simply a place.

To carry out the reordering Raggi had to confront the problem of the physical limits to the distribution, a permanent obstacle to opening up and maintaining the internal perspectives. Raggi opted for diversity, using various methods of organization that would afford a multi-faceted and changing view of the same reality. He used sliding doors, and the walls served a two fold function as partitions and as furniture. Through this system the rooms can be either separate or connected spaces, depending on the needs of the moment.

At the express wish of the owner, a section was designed for work, a study in which to store books and documents. In the former layout this new study used to be a bedroom. The living room remained in the same space because of its communicating outdoor terraces. In the new arrangement, the larger rooms (the dining room, the living room and the study) occupy a considerable proportion of the total space, and can assume different aspects depending on the position of the architectural barriers. From the basis of the qualitative factor of variability, multiple readings of the same physical space are possible.

The rest of the distribution follows rational lines. The new bedroom is located in part of the old service area and, along with the main bathroom and the communicating corridor, occupies the rear section of the floor plan. The kitchen remained in its original position, but now a greater number of functions is concentrated in

The wooden section of the surface shown in the photo on the right folds down to reveal a small display alcove.

One of the two cabinets that flank the door from the dining-room into the corridor which leads to the bedroom.

a smaller space (an additional toilet and a small guest room). This new layout places greater importance on the living space and reduces domestic needs, without neglecting functional efficiency.

The interior decor reflects the architect's desire to lend a special ambience to each of the sections: the main or collective space, the rest area and the service area. However, each reflects the basic principle of the planning and execution: a return to techniques with a craftsman-like quality, the objective being to draw architectural values closer to those of interior design and ornamentation. This is one of the reasons why the constructed boundaries serve a twofold functional and aesthetic purpose, acting as furniture inspired by the forms of architecture. No element is gratuitous, with the exception of the moulding used throughout the apartment, which expresses conceptual and historical referents.

In the hall Raggi's characteristic affinities are first observed. On the right side of the entrance is a small curving wall, which, in addition to constituting a highly expressive gesture, screens the coat rack from view. On the white wall is one of the plaster fragments, simulating an Ionic column, executed with various components, that attempts to suggest a memory of the residence itself in a highly evocative paradox. Facing the entrance, a small piece of furniture against the wall establishes the transition to the dining room and offers two different fronts. It is executed in cedarwood, with a rectangular mirror facing the door and a blue marble shelf.

Preliminary sketch for one corner of the dining room; in the definitive design the tiling was replaced with marble.

Preliminary sketch of the wall between the living room and the study.

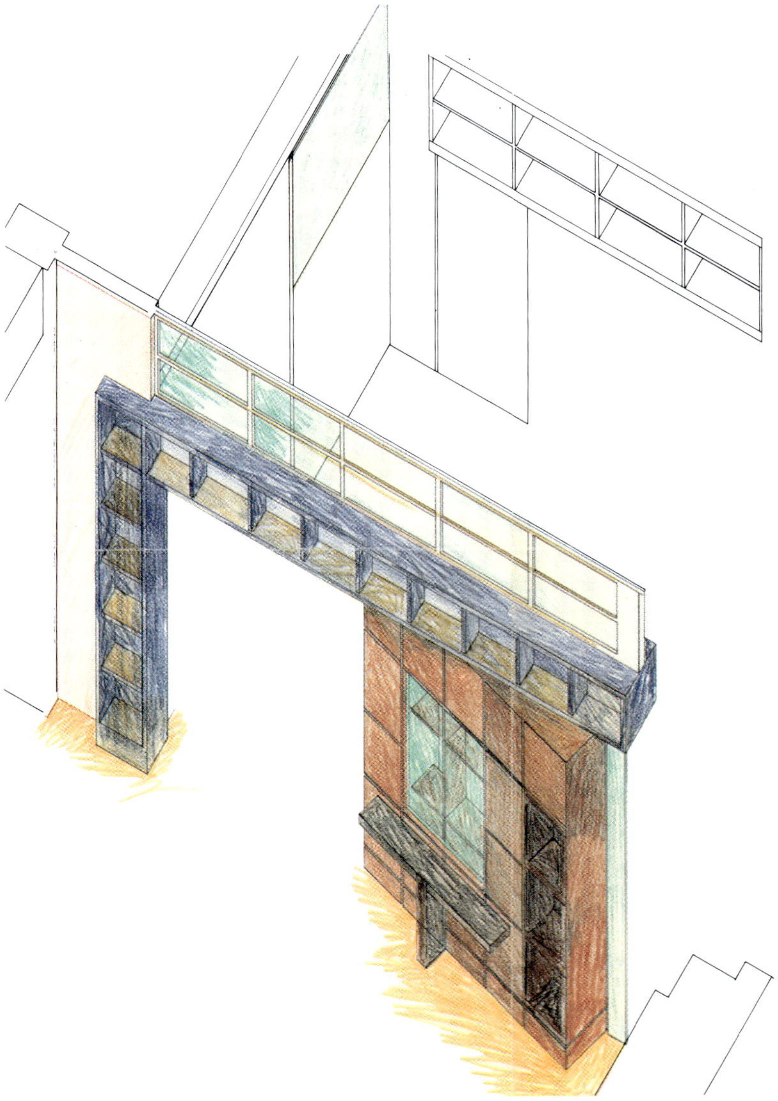

The entrance hall offers direct access to the kitchen, the living room and the dining room. The latter is a new space and its most significant value in the layout is its connection with the bedroom and the study. The far wall of the dining room has a door with two sliding wings that close to form a central square. It is executed in cedarwood and can function as a shelf. Both sections are finished with an opaque lacquer. A singlewing sliding door provides access to the work room. The door is concealed behind a large plate of pink Portogallo marble, with a console in cedarwood and stainless steel and two rectangular openings in the upper section. Embedded in the cedar are fragments of beechwood, forming an arrow-like directional symbol.

The strategies employed to create the study are also based on the fusion of architecture and furniture. The room was conceived as a continuous series of concave shelves that surround the entire perimeter. The significant aspect of this room is its method of communication with the living room. The two spaces are divided by a large wood partition wall with a concealed sliding door. Its unique features are the direction of the planes (their meeting is oblique because of the inclination of the partition), the panelling of the exterior frame (lacquered in cobalt blue) and a second appearance of the sign of the arrow, this time on the door panel. The contrast in colour and direction dominates its bold, expressive design. Depending on the position of the door, the study and the living room can form one vast undivided space.

Regarding the materials and decorative elements,

American cedar is used throughout and the flooring is of Siam teak. In the corridor between the bedroom and the bath there is a luxurious carpet that lends the space the improbable air of a grand hotel. This corridor is finished in green and contains several built-in closets. Most of the furniture and decorative elements are products of prominent designers: Piero Castiglioni's Sillaba lamp for Fontana Arte is in the entrance and there is a Bastiano divan by the Scarpas for Knoll in the library. To complete this brief description, another mention must be made of the plaster fragments and mouldings inspired by various stimuli, which enhance the quality of the setting and constitute a gesture evoking a fictitious and unreal history, illustrating the tremendous suggestive power of Raggi's language.

View from the study into the living room; with the door fully open, the two spaces become one.

In this project the Milanese architect has demonstrated his undeniable skill in spatial interpretation and his unique conception of interior design, based on a return to craftsmanship in the realms of furniture and decoration. Imbuing these fields with architectural values is the most noteworthy accomplishment of this project, which also enjoys the benefits of the aptness and narrative economy of Franco Raggi's designs.

The basic idea behind the renovation was to make the house functional.

Remodelling an old farmhouse

Julie Phipps & Peter Cook

This old French farmhouse, built around 1870, is situated in the heart of the countryside in a wine-producing area called Domaine de Gaillac. The area is characterised by strong prevailing winds, but the woods in front of the house protect it from them. The designer and photographer Julie Phipps and her companion Peter Cook bought the house in 1987 with the intention of using it as a summer residence. As it had only been empty for two months, they expected to be able to move in immediately. They soon discovered, however, that they were in possession of an old farmhouse without electricity or plumbing. It was plain that it needed a complete remodelling job – indeed a almost a reconstruction – to transform the farmhouse into a home.

Julie Phipps' true vocation is photography, but throughout her career she has also dedicated herself to fashion design, a hobby that led her to start a clothing business in 1972 to manufacture and sell her own designs. Despite the enormous success of this business, she gave it up in order to pursue her true interest and study documentary photography for two years at the Newport College of Art. The knowledge she acquired there gave her a solid base for her photographic work. Since 1983, she has specialised in architecture and interior design photography, and currently receives commissions from architects and specialised magazines in England and the United States.

Julie Phipps is neither an architect nor an interior designer; however, she undertook the remodelling of this residence herself. As she designed the house for her own

In the kitchen, Julie Phipps decided to paint the walls a strong blue.

Detail of a room beside the kitchen showing mosaic of different-coloured tiles on the floor.

personal use and that of their family, the basic idea behind the work was to make it functional and suitable for use as a holiday home, the owner wanted it to be bright, sunny and a place in which colour played an important part. In this region, where the climate favours outdoor living, the garden is also an important part of the house and had to be given special attention. Although a part of the original property had been sold to local farmers, the house still stands in two and a half acres of land. The garden was planned to provide spaces for rest and recreation; paths cut through the rough meadow and plenty of open space for football, tennis, etc., were all part of the plan. The swimming pool has its own garden surrounded by classic French ironwork. Seen from outside, the farmhouse is still classically French, although this renovation project has meant that the interior design comes as a great surprise.

The original farmhouse was long, which gave it a marvellous angle of view. However, as is common in old houses, the windows were few and narrow. The layout of the house was also unsuitable for the needs of a modern family; there was little light coming from the outside; the main access opened directly into the living room; the dining room was non existent; and the kitchen was too big, having been designed in accordance with the old tradition of centring family life in this room.

The original doors and floor tiles in the farmhouse were not worth restoring, so Julie Phipps and Peter Cook decided to modify the existing layout and give the whole house a fresh appearance. They tried to ensure the

On the upper floor the rustic look is enhanced by the bare wood of the beams.

entrance of natural light from the exterior, and opted for a simple combination of bright colours on the interior walls to avoid disorder and confusion. Their intention was that the whole house should be chosen rather than inherited.

Light is a very important aspect in this house. The original building had no window on the walls at each end as these areas were used for housing animals and storing hay. The small openings which existed were very narrow and barely let in the sunlight. In all, eight large picture windows were put in, guaranteeing not only natural light and ventilation, but also opening up a pleasant view of the surrounding landscape from every part of the house.

Although each room is different, the relationship between them has been established by the colour scheme. Soft colours were chosen to smooth out the rough edges and distemper was used for the walls of the different rooms since it allows the plaster to breathe and gives a feeling of natural colouring rather than a skin.

In the kitchen, Julie Phipps decided to paint the walls a strong blue, which she says is a colour she associates with France. In the bedrooms, light shades predominate: cream and white, in order to emphasise the light coming in from outside.

In a house designed as a second residence for holidays and short stays during the year, everything should be practical, accessible, and designed to minimise

Although all the rooms are different the overall decoration is unified through the use of light colours on the walls.

View of the bedroom. Soft colours were chosen to smooth out the rough edges.

time and effort; for this reason, the bathrooms were designed as functional rooms and the kitchen is equipped with modern appliances. The whole interior is suited to the needs of a modern family.

The interior decorators added an amusing touch with the "Dr. Glob" dining-room chairs designed by Philippe Stark; they provide a little modern touch in sharp contrast to the antique wooden table, bought locally, which harmonises with the original atmosphere of the house. The "Dr. Glob" chairs add a little counterpoint to the main living room and the dining room of the house.

The remodelling of this old farmhouse to transform it into a residence respected the native architecture and design; all the building work was carried out by local French craftsmen. Even the paint on the walls was bought locally. Only in the garden, where the aim was also to maintain the French style, a few aspects of English life were introduced, such as the shady areas where traditional picnics can be organised.

View of the living area showing the stove and the first-floor gallery.

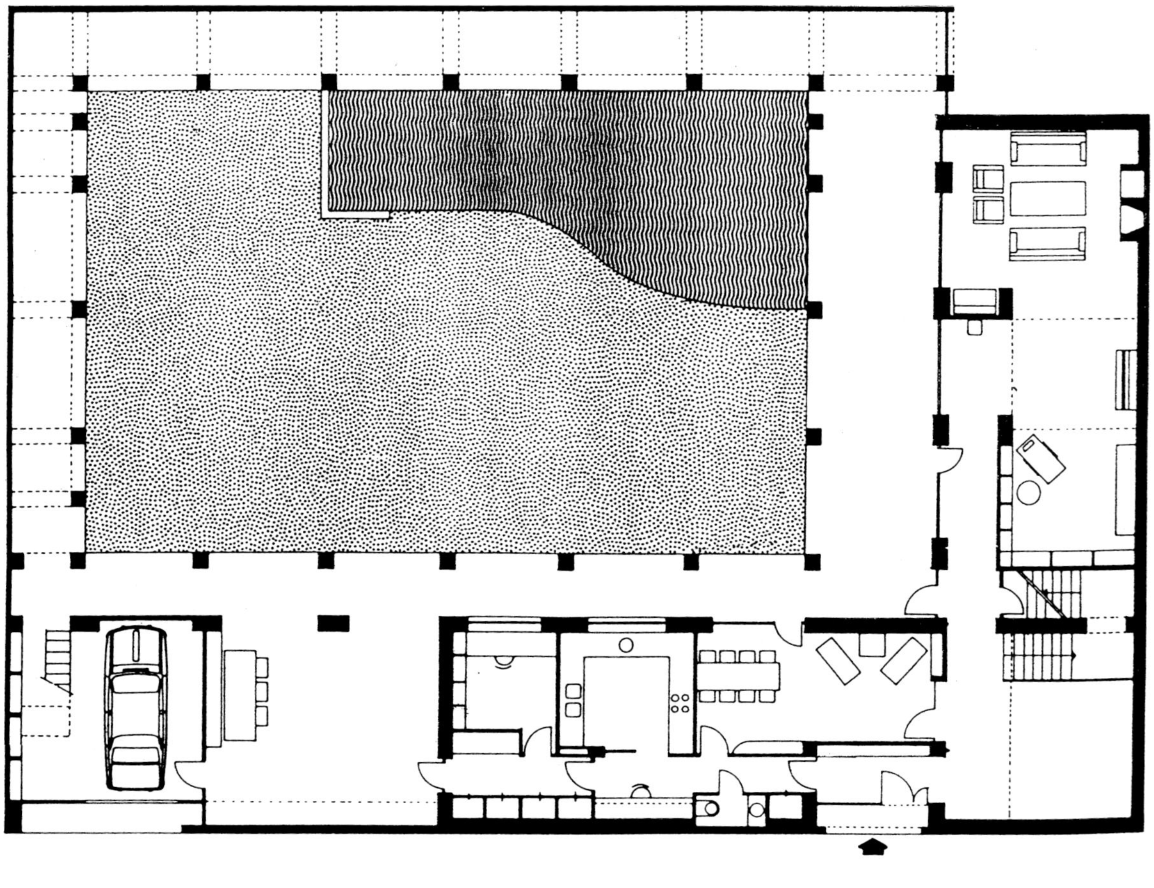

Ground plan of the whole property.

Interior views

Antonio Vila Ramis

Taking as his point of departure a pre-existing architectural studio and an adjacent available plot. Tono Vila conceived the idea of a house and a leisure area adjoining the site of the original building. The house is on the Mediterranean island of Majorca, where the light and the climate of the area play a dominant role. The district was created in the Town Planning Ordinance of 1920 for the outlying villages of the town. Today this area is a virtual suburb but it has maintained its peaceful, residential ambience, with the pine grove of a convent and the bell tower of the parish church in the vicinity. The building regulations of this district stipulate continuous construction between party walls and the alignment of the facade with the street.

Constrained by these conditions and intending to achieve complete intimacy and privacy, Tono Vila decided on a closed block with no windows facing the street, the ground plan coinciding with the boundaries of the plot, thereby conforming to the building regulations governing the site.

Antonio Vila Ramis was born in Palma de Mallorca in 1948. In 1973 he was awarded a degree in Architecture from the Escuela Técnica Superior de Arquitectura in Barcelona. This polyglot architect (Spanish, Catalan, French, Italian, English and Swedish) was awarded a grant by I.A.E.S.T.E. for an internship with Bourekas Architects in Athens, Greece (1971), and later with the Taisei Construction Company in Osaka, Japan (1972). Vila was director of the Guillem Sagrera Historical Archives of C.O.A.B., Balearics Division, where he was chiefly involved in the inventory, cataloguing and protection of the architectural, town planning and landscaping tradition of the Balearic Islands (1976-1978). He was also director of Exhibitions and Lectures of the Balearics Division of the C.O.A.B. (1980-83), and of the editorial board of the study "Commercial Land for the integrated Commercial Development Programme in the Balearics" (1981), and director of the Urban Design Office for Town Planning in Palma (1982). In 1985 he taught a course in landscape architecture, and was cultural activities coordinator of the Balearic Islands Official College of Architects (1987). His professional career has included the construction, refurbishment, restoration and enlargement of numerous residences, several projects for green zones and gardens, the design and paving of streets and public squares and of the Palma ring road extension. He has also planned and organised exhibitions, delivered stimulating lectures, participated in several congresses and received several awards. All these activities and honours have contributed to his growing reputation.

The ground plan of the complex is square, with dimensions identical to those of the site. It contains several buildings: the architecture studio (already in existence at the outset), the guest area and the residence itself, all arranged along the perimeter to enclose a central area of courtyards and gardens. The house is L-shaped, and its vertex forms an inner court roofed by a skylight, which acts as the linking module of the different units and spaces.

The building has two distinct floors. On the right-hand side of the ground floor are the dining room, the kitchen and its facilities, the porch and the garage. The living room is on the left. After climbing a staircase, the visitor enters a recreation room which opens onto a balcony overlooking the courtyard or patio.

The first floor is divided into two separate areas: on the right is the children's section, with their bedrooms, dressing rooms, bathrooms and terrace. The left is reserved for the parents, with a master bedroom, dressing room and bathroom. The separation between parents and children and the privacy of each is clearly respected. All these rooms have views of the spacious interior garden. The original studio also has a bedroom and bathroom which may be occupied by guests. The architect Tono Vila intended to design a single space

Floor plan of the building.

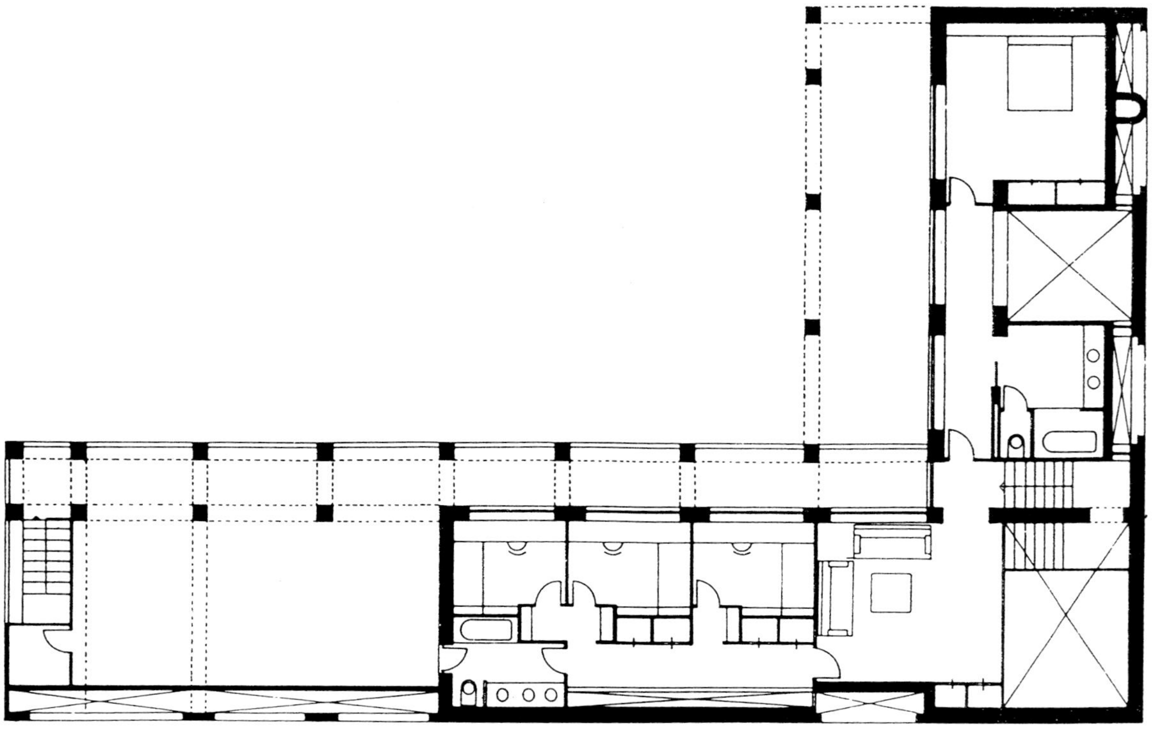

View of the lounge. For the connections of the various rooms, the traditional system has been used in their construction.

where work, rest and leisure activities would be fully compatible.

The six-metre exterior wall serves as the street facade. However, to accentuate the vitality of the architect's conception, the perimeter wall surrounding the grounds was finished with very smooth ochre stucco, acting as the outer skin of what we might call the body of the house. This wall, or protective skin, has several openings which allow light to enter and hint at the existence of private living space behind it.

The technique of enclosing the residence with walls following the periphery created architectural problems of light and ventilation which Vila solved by means of skylights, transoms and other elements.

The living room is decorated in a variety of restful natural tones.

Hallway leading to the lounge. The tiles are of fired clay.

Section of the building.

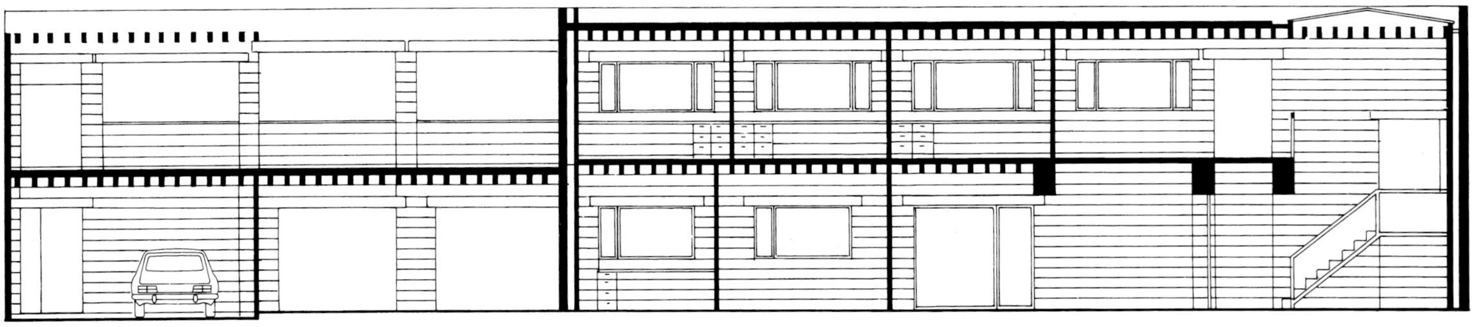

The architect's wish to settle down on the island and to express his respect and admiration for it is evident from the inclusion of the atrium and the courtyard, a Roman/Arabic legacy in residential building which became firmly rooted in Majorca. His regard is also apparent in the use of materials traditionally used in Majorcan constructions. He has employed them as direct contrasts to the of life expressed in the garden (the water, the plants and the occupants).

The principal materials used in the complex are compact sandstone (a local stone known as Marés), potter's clay tiles and wood. The conventional dimensions of the Marés (40 x 80 cm) formed the module defining the proportions of the house. These building modules are accentuated in the composition of the paving.

The architect was able to give free rein to his imagination in the design of the lighting. He was well aware of the effects to be achieved with the shadows and reflections which light would create in the various spaces, and he attempted to modulate and filter it in harmony with the different rooms and their functions. He intended the interior light to indicate the passage of time.

Regarding the materials, another noteworthy feature of the design is the flat roof, insulated and weather-proofed, and covered with earthenware tiles. Both the interior flooring and exterior paving were executed in 20 x 20 cm earthenware tiles, except for the playroom on the first floor which is floored with matchboard of northern wood fixed on fillets. The exterior and interior walls are of exposed Marés masonry, except for the perimeter wall,

which is covered both inside and out with a rough coat of Portland cement and a finish of lime and cement, tinted by the addition of washed clays.

The exposed prestressed beams of the ceilings are painted white. The kitchen, bathrooms and toilet are faced in Iberian travertine marble. The bathroom furniture is Roca Gondola and the fittings are Vola, designed by Arne Jacobsen. To bind the various elements a traditional technique was applied. The mortar used for laying the stones was a mixture of natural cement, gripi *and sand from the same stone.*

Clearly, the exterior wall/facade successfully isolates the house from the surrounding environment. Rapport with nature was developed through the internal life of the garden, dominated by the blue of the irregular swimming pool and by the orange trees. The architect has thus achieved withdrawal which never signifies darkness or sorrow. The entire complex, where work and pleasure coexist in peaceful harmony, is bursting with life, light and colour. The house only turns its back on the immediate setting in order to achieve true privacy and intimacy. The complex has deep roots in the earth and is adapted to the traditions and peculiarities of this unique island, respecting its history and its natural environment.

The rooms are decorated with works by such celebrated artists as Miró, Calder, Albers and Stella, which are offset by the neutral setting, in which the leather chairs designed by Mies van der Rohe and Le Corbusier accentuate the classic style of this residence.

The dining room opens onto the interior patio's large garden.

The mortar used for the borders is a mixture of ***gripi*** and sand from the same stone.

The units are arranged as a perimeter, and enclose a central area of various patios and gardens.

Perspective drawing of the interior staircase.

Monumental architecture in an everyday setting

Sergio Puente & Ada Dewes

This construction rises up out of the Mexican countryside like a Toltecan pyramid, faithful to its idiosyncratic setting. It is a single-family dwelling near the small district of San Bernabe in Mexico City, and it is the property of the architects who built it. They are a husband-and-wife team – she is German and he Mexican. In fact, it is this mixture of radically different cultures and origins which has helped to create a genuine Mexican temple, with a lead-grey interior flooded with sunlight.

The house is situated on a hilltop just outside what could possibly be called the outer limits of Mexico City. The site was chosen for its peacefulness and its close proximity to the city. While the characteristics of the site dictated the architectural structure, it was actually chosen for the very characteristics which made this design possible. The architects wanted to construct the building fairly high up, taking into account the elevation of Mexico City, and also wanted to locate their residence at some distance from its noise and bustle. From this house the occupants have a clear view of Mexico City, like a fleeting first impression: a vast sea of houses illuminated at night by a network of lights stretching off into the horizon on a flat plain bordered in the distance by volcanoes.

Ada Dewes was born in Germany in 1944. She obtained her degree in Graphic Design, studying from 1960 to 1964 in the Products and Communication Design Faculty of Hannover's Werkkunstschule. She spent the next two years studying painting in the Arts Academy in Berlin. Her earnest desire to be in a position to defend the theory of design and painting led her to study

Detail of a terrace with mosaic flooring showing the cylindrical support column.

Various elevations of the house.

linguistics in Mexico from 1973 to 1977. She eventually obtained a doctorate in General Semantics and Visual Semeiotics in 1973 from the École des Hautes Études en Sciences Sociales in Paris, awarded after submission of her thesis on contemporary avant-garde movements. Since 1975 she has taught in the School of Arts and Sciences in Mexico City's Universidad Autónoma Metropolitana, lecturing on Visual Semeiotics and the Semeiotics of Space. She has carried out research into visual language and semantic mechanisms in pictorial and architectural texts, with particular reference to postmodern architecture. She applies semeiotics to design in general, and especially to architectural design. She has lived for long periods in Berlin, London, Paris, Iviza and Mexico.

Sergio Puente was born in Mexico City in 1942. He obtained his degree from the School of Architecture in Mexico City's Universidad Autónoma Metropolitana. Between 1969 and 1970 he undertook postgraduate studies in architecture and town planning in the Architectural Association School of Architects in London. He continued his studies in the School of Environmental Studies in London's University College and in 1972 he was awarded an M.Sc. in Architecture and Town Planning. These studies were further enhanced at the École des Hautes Études en Sciences Sociales in Paris, where he obtained a doctorate in 1982 in Local Planning and Regional Analysis. Since 1975 he has been a lecturer in the School of Arts and Sciences in Mexico City's Universidad Autónoma Metropolitana, and since 1980

View of the dining room with French windows, showing the large cylindrical black column on the left.

Section of the house.

Living area, where the spaciousness is emphasised by the interplay of cold colours.

has also lectured at the Centre for Demographic and Urban Studies in the same city. In 1990 and 1991 he was guest lecturer at the University of Paris IV (the Sorbonne), where he taught doctoral courses on town and regional planning.

The building takes the form of a pyramid reminiscent of an Aztec temple. The surroundings have been echoed in the architecture by means of the contrast of the structural axes. The house was designed on the premise of its principal inherent features: an airy house open to the sky above with well placed views, and open transversely towards the cactus garden. The main construction axis projects upwards by means of a central glass ceiling which gives it a conservatory-like appearance. It also turns the empty space between the

Plans of various levels.

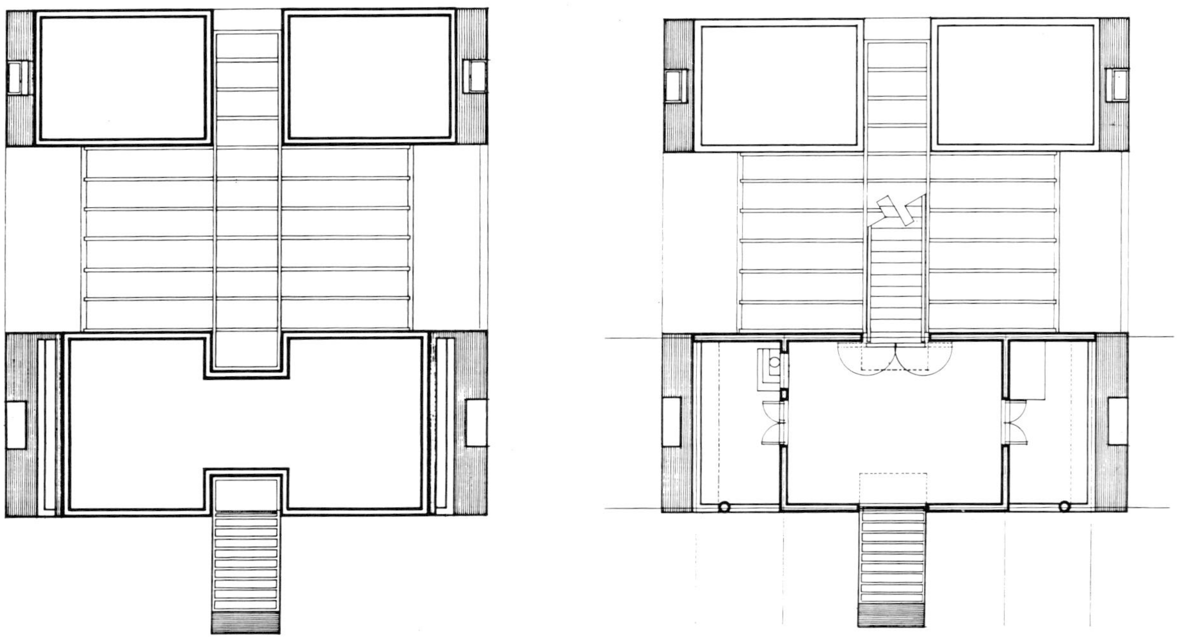

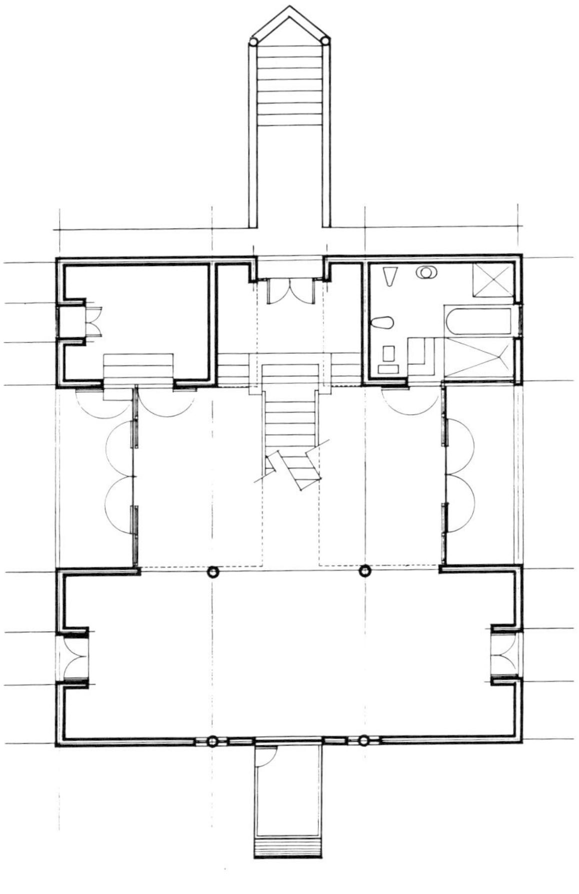

View of the staircase which custs through the dwelling at a right angle. The first three steps are paved and the remainder are wooden.

The bedroom is an attic room with sloping windows. The bed base is made of solid wood.

various units into useful space and links interior to exterior. The main elevation is nevertheless closed off to the street and surrounding buildings by this central axis, thus protecting the interior.

The elevation providing access to the dwelling is a compact concrete block with a central glass door which constitutes the axial structure. This central axis is further emphasised by the exterior wooden staircase leading into the house. The staircase cuts through the dwelling at a right angle and leads to the aviary. In the upper section, it leads to a sloping window commanding a view of passing clouds and the surrounding countryside. This window also functions as a roof above the bed and as a point of entry for sunlight. This imaginary line follows the north-south axis, so that the dwelling's central axis is aligned with the points of the compas, the various spaces indicating the time of day like a huge sundial. This symmetry and the interior layout create what seems to be a circular space, determining the day-to-day appearance of the structure.

In homage to the link between their family life and their animals, Ada Dewes and Sergio Puente decided that the large number of animals living in the house should be reflected in its architecture. A house framing the sky above required birds, and for this reason an aviary was built as a visual continuation of the lounge. To the same end a water mirror was provided for the ducks in the rectangle which makes up the ground floor plan.

The kitchen and bathroom are both extremely clearly defined and functional spaces. These large units, totally

Drawing of the main elevation of the house and its surroundings.

separate from the rest, are really houses within a single house. The kitchen is in shade where the roofs slope down, and in comparison the bathroom is flooded with light. The staircase leads up to the bedroom, which is enclosed by a suspended door. This room was designed as an attic, and its sloping windows intersect at right angles to each other at an imaginary point in space. The terraces leading outside enhance the effect of this imaginary structure.

In order to create the effect of total mutual dependence and continuity between interior and exterior, the colours used outside were continued to the interior. A small amount of white, relegated for so long to being a background, regains its role as a colour or non-colour, making the interior seem more spacious, as it is

A touch of nostalgia in the kitchen: the geometric layout of the tiles.

Details evocative of the past in the bathroom, such as the mirror with geometric shapes.

Mirror subdivided into geometric shapes and wooden ornaments in an interior decorated with cold colours.

continually reflected in the glass surfaces and chilly colours. In the garden, however, which has been left to grow wild, the dominant colour is a pale shade of faded yellow.

It was the intention of the two architects to include features reminiscent of the past, evoking the passage of time. The old staircase was placed at the centre of the house, and is an elegant wooden structure which functions as a link between inside and outside, the top of the house and the bottom. The mosaics also conjure up the past and, like the other components, were designed specifically for this house. There are other reminders of the past around the house – the all-marble bathroom, the mirror subdivided into geometric shapes and also the geometric layout of the kitchen tiling.

Looking at this structure, one gets the impression that the contrast between nature and culture was the main factor generating the architecture of the project: open spaces, closed spaces, bright spaces and shady corners, the lightness of a glass construction fusing the separate solid units anchored to the ground by their pyramidal shape. Ada Dewes and Sergio Puente set out to enlarge everyday features in a kind of architectural ritual, thus making good their escape from the human scale, which tends to create structures made in man's image. Here even the functions of the various rooms – the kitchen and bathroom, for instance – are playfully and pleasurably reinterpreted.

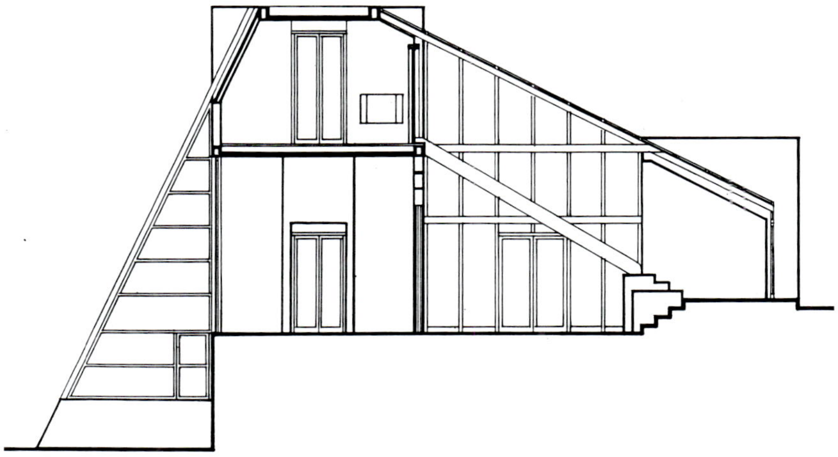

The dwelling's east elevation.

West elevation of the house, taking in the original main entrance.

Modern forms added

Hinrich Storch & Walter Ehlers

This construction by Hinrich Storch and Walter Ehlers stemmed from the remodelling of a house which had to be converted, with alterations to its original structure. This did not mean, however, that new forms could not be superimposed or certain cumbersome aspects changed.

The house, one of a row of houses, is situated in the German city of Hanover, on a site in Kleiner Hillen Street. The land on which the old house was built had no particular feature relevant to the project, and looked onto the street and garden, the basic reference points for orienting the new construction.

Hinrich Storch was born in Berlin in 1933. He was trained in higher technical studies in Brunswick between 1954 and 1961. He continued his practical studies in Zonguldak (Turkey) in 1958, which enabled him to travel in Europe, the Middle East and North Africa. He set up the Heier & Monse studio in Cologne. A professor at Oesterlen, Hanover, and assistant scientist at the Brunswick Higher School, he has had his own studio, with Walter Ehlers, in Hanover since 1964.

Walter Ehlers, born in 1936, was educated in Holzminden and later attended the Higher Technical School in Munich (1955-1958) and the Higher Technical School in Brunswick (1958-1962). He continued his practical training in Stockholm and travelled in Europe and the Middle East. He worked at the Oesterlen studio in Hanover, and has had his own studio in partnership with Hinrich Storch since 1964. He was president of the BDA (Association of German Architects) from 1977 to 1983, and has been vice-president of the same organisation since 1987.

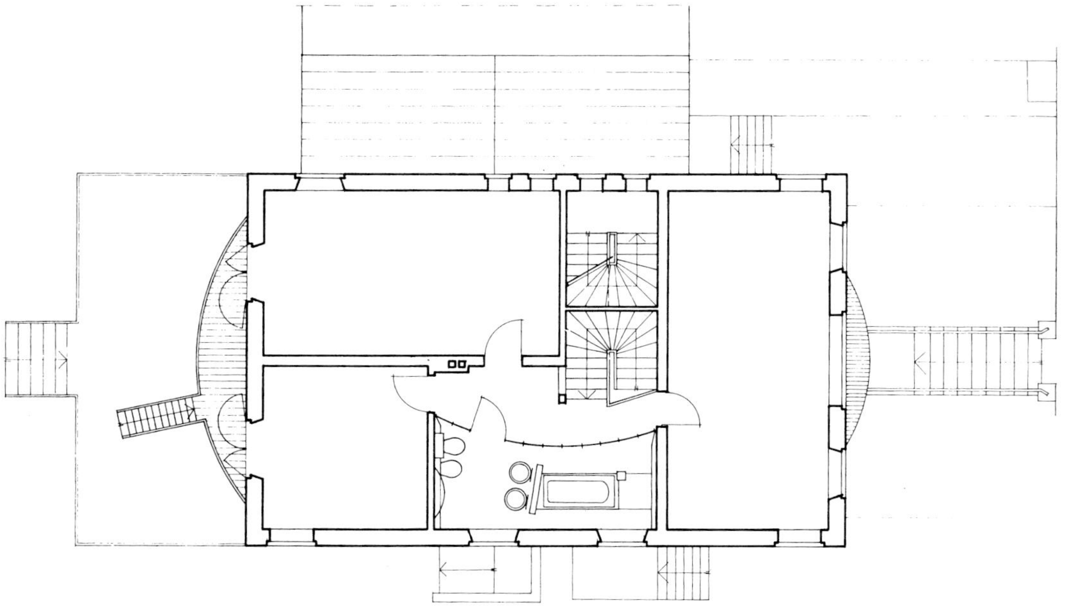

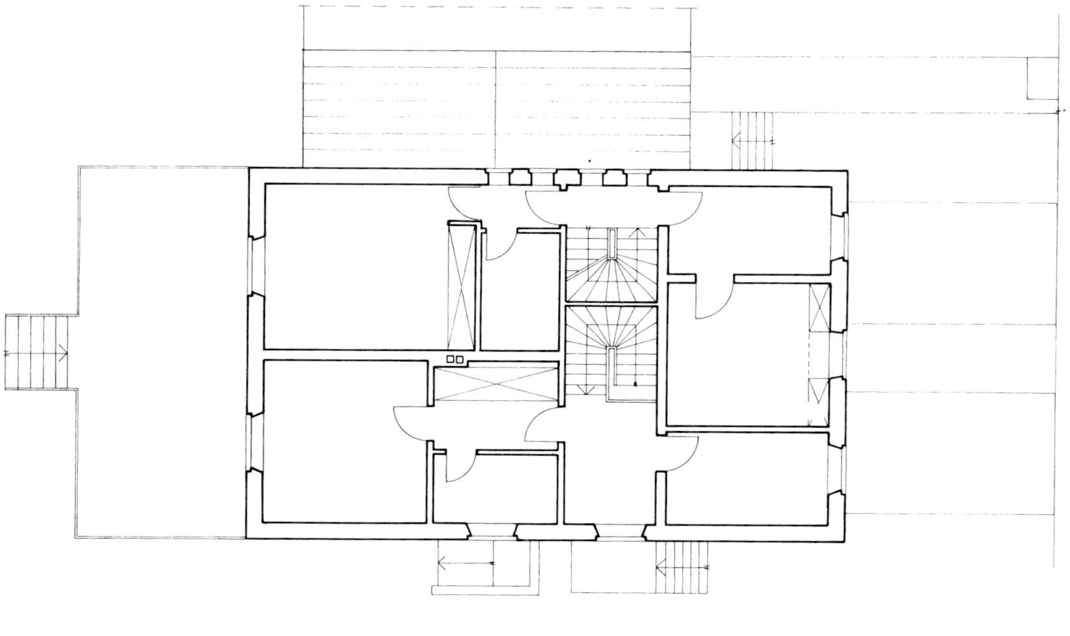

The building was constructed on a rectangular plan; it has two separate floors and a rented apartment in the attic which is completely independent. The ground floor contains the reception and family rooms, whilst the bedrooms are located on the first floor. The front door on one side of the house opens onto the hall where the kitchen is situated. On the same floor there is a living room (with a semi-circular hearth in the middle of the room), a library, dining room and a large terrace opening onto the garden. The master bathroom and bedrooms are on the first floor, together with a large studio. The bedrooms on the first floor have direct access to the garden from a balcony and stairway. The house also has a spacious garage.

Storch and Ehlers decided to concentrate on the sheltering aspects and functions of the house, which

Plans of the first and ground floors respectively.

The curved chimney is attached to a prismatic unit. The dining room captures light through the windows in the upper corner.

Steel structures recall the original shape of the house – this structure on the ceiling of the lounge, for example.

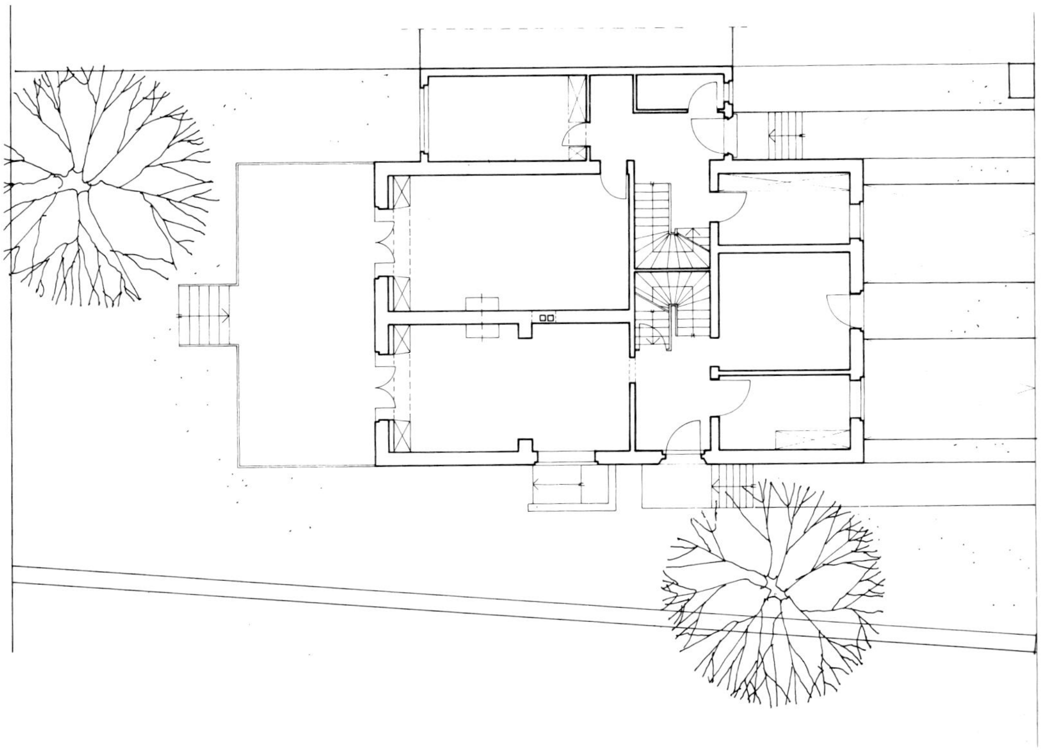

Plan of the lower level.

Elevation leading to the street.

Elevation leading to the garden.

The painting room required special lighting, and for this reason it has a large window opening onto the street.

would affect its original form: insulation to conserve heat, weather-proofing, etc. The result is a compact building with pitched roofs designed for rain-water drainage and climatically suited to the region.

The functions of the various rooms and floors also determined the final appearance of the house. The area converted into a painter's studio needed special lighting and has a large window looking out over the street. One unusual aspect in terms of functionality is, without a doubt, the kitchen, which is located in the entrance hall. Both architects agreed that the concept of a kitchen separated from the rest of the house was an oldfashioned idea no longer relevant today. They also considered, from personal experience, that a screen was not necessary, as the room was big enough to be able to get around problems of extreme temperatures and draughts. It was also built at a slightly oblique angle and in the opposite direction to the wind, and sheltered by a small glass partition. The entrance area could therefore be kept large and open. The top bedrooms, however, were to be linked to the garden by an added balcony and stairway.

The relationship of the house to its location was affected by two fundamental points of reference: the street and the garden. The original building, in any event, was not altogether suited to the way it was situated. The most attractive facade did not face the front, but rather faced the eastern, less significant side. The new entrance, with the sculptural effect of the stairway, the dropped eaves and the studio window redirected the house towards the street. The balcony performed the

The indoor stairs lead directly to the opaque glass wall of the bathroom.

View of the hallway, the dining room and the staircase. In the foreground, the pillars separating this area from the kitchen.

The children's room leads into the garden and features children's motifs on its furniture.

same function on the garden side, and in this way reinforced and accentuated the role of the terrace in the old house. After these alterations the eastern side now plays a less significant role and looks less ostentatious, thanks to the windows positioned at either end of the building.

Another factor the architects considered important was the lighting. Apart from sunlight, the architects considered it important that the inhabitants enjoy the movement of the sun, which is why the windows are positioned at the top corners of each room. The staircase and corridor are also not only artificially lit but are also bathed in light from the windows set in the wall beside the front door.

Both Storch and Ehlers were convinced that the method of construction should be directly related to the building's requirements, and that the materials, being natural resources, ought to be used with care. Constructions using few materials are, as a general rule, the most expressive and subtle. Here the choice of materials has largely been governed by the functional criteria. It was therefore necessary to incorporate steel elements to liven up the original appearance of the house.

The same principle applied to the plate glass wall and warped steel in the bathroom; without this curve the space would have been too small and has thus been enlarged. It is true that the additional steel structures gave a new look to the building, but this has not been done without a degree of sensitivity towards the original appearance. The new elements are handcrafted, subtle and concise, and the materials have been used extremely sparingly.

Bathroom, with steel and glass wall to the left and bath to the rear.

The front door to the house, the window, the dropped eaves, balcony, outside staircase and the pilasters, all added by Storch and Ehlers, make a unity of connected forms which endow this architectural structure with a noticeably new appearance.

The main aim of the work was to establish these forms, but they were used as concisely as possible. Nevertheless, the bold contrasts between the traditional architectural techniques used in the original construction and the new construction methods do not clash; on the contrary, the result is totally coherent, harmonious and in keeping with the original form.

The kitchen, with its unusual, functional appearance, is located in the hallway.

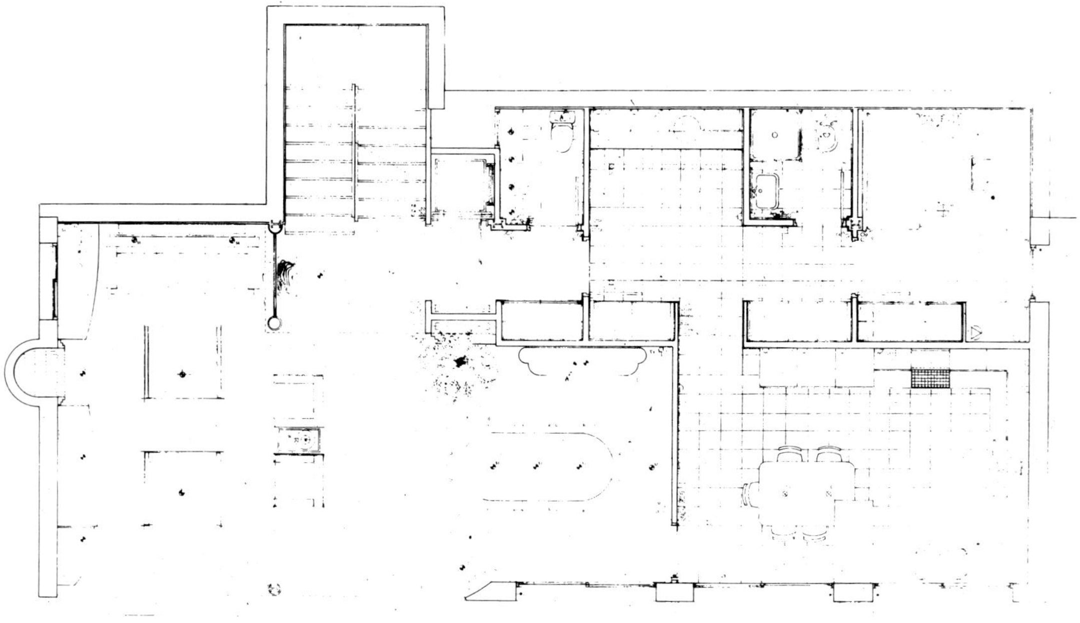

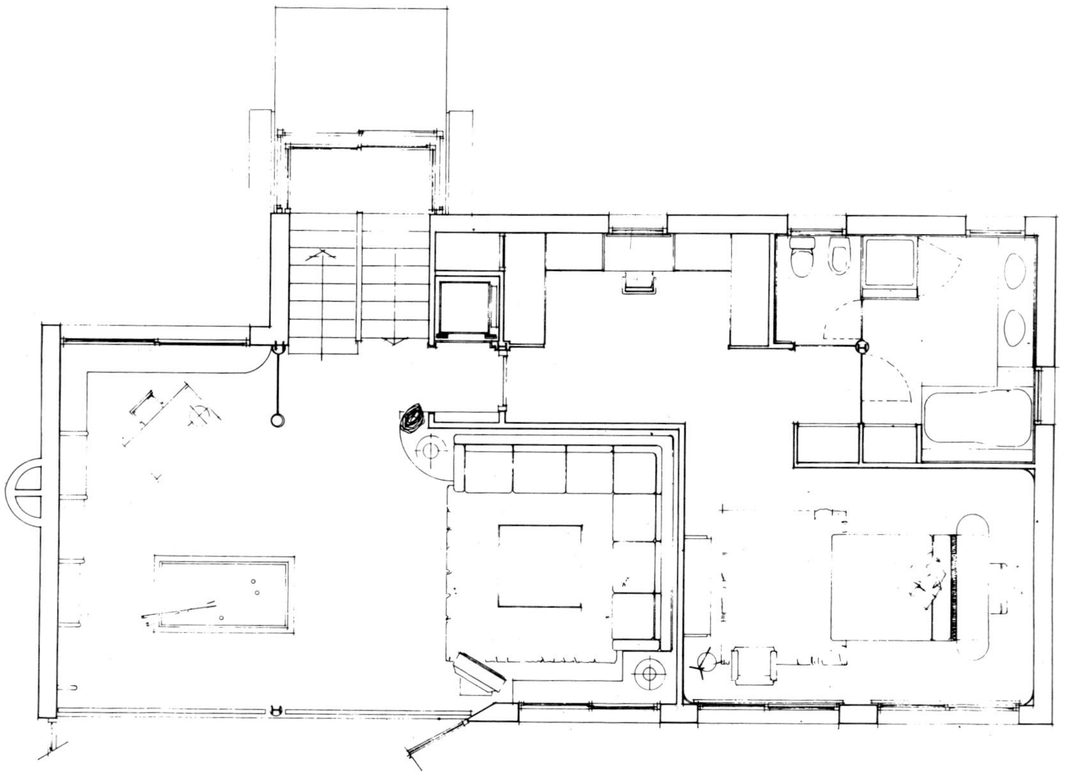

Plan of the lower level.

Plan of the upper level.

Unified vertical glazing

Joan Maria Pascual

The design for this house by Joan Maria Pascual was planned according to the needs and demands of its owners. However, in addition to this functional aspect, great care and attention were paid to details of the interior design, which was undertaken by the prestigious interior designers Ernest Ameller and Xavier Prats.

The house is located in the upper district of Barcelona on a steeply sloping site. The building has been intelligently adapted to the topographical features of the land, and offers magnificent views over the city.

The P/S/P company consists of Joan Maria Pascual i Cañellas and Ferrán de los Santos i Arnau. The firm has taken a professional approach to its work since its foundation in 1969 and, apart from the senior architects mentioned above, also has a senior collaborating architect, a surveyor, two draughtsmen and a secretary. The basic team is made up of seven people who work with the latest computer design equipment. Moreover, the group collaborates with various technical offices and specialist studios as a multidisciplinary team. Estudio P/S/P has had broad experience covering various fields from interior design to town planning, and in the domain of architecture this includes the design of housing, offices, industrial buildings, hospitals, rehabilitation centres, hotels, schools, shopping centres, etc.. They are currently working on plans and site management for a building development covering a total surface area of 215,000 m^2. They have held several exhibitions, have had articles published in journals and their work has won them a number of prizes.

The poolroom area is on the upper floor and provides a splendid view of Barcelona.

Ernest Ameller (Barcelona, 1949) and Xavier Prats (Barcelona, 1943) carried out the interior design of this house. The former studied in Bordeaux and started work as an interior designer on returning to his native city. In 1979 he was involved in designing furniture and objects for several companies in Barcelona. Xavier Prats, having specialised in interior decor, upholstery, furniture and design applications, set up his own company which specialised in design projects. Their association led, in 1986, to the founding of Interdos, an interior decor and design studio. They have undertaken both public and private projects throughout Spain: Vichy Catalán, Clínica Barraquer and hotels such as the Rancho, Playafels, Andorra Palace, Bañacrisi, etc.

The three-storey house was constructed on an

The sofas in the lounge are ***alcantara*** and the floor has been executed in ***merbau*** parquet.

irregular ground plan. Two storeys have a glazed uniform wall, with a garage on the other floor. A stairway links the three floors and is supplemented by a small lift. The ground floor includes a kitchen and two large living rooms, open to the exterior as a result of the plate glass wall, which overlook the swimming pool. The layout of the first floor includes four bedrooms, each with a bathroom suite and a small work area. The billiard and games room on the top floor has a splendid view over Barcelona. Ouutside, the house is surrounded by a terraced garden which, like the built-in swimming pool, follows the exact contours of the land.

One of the principal concerns of the studio was the lighting. The light and warmth so typical of the Mediterranean have been exploited to the full and make

the interior bright and cheerful all year round.

The huge plate glass wall plays a major role in the building and there are a large number of other windows set into the facades; hence the interior is closely linked to the exterior. The garden and greenery outdoors are reflected in the glass and it makes it seem as though there are no physical barriers between. The desire to join both worlds comes over also in the construction of the swimming pool, which has been built as a part of the structure of the house.

There is also a feeling of cohesion inside the house. General finishes have been chosen for their uniformity. The flooring and staircases are all in parquet which has been stained the same colour throughout, whereas the doors and furniture are all in beige. The Carrara marble fireplace matches the three worktops, constructed in the same material used as supports for the sofas. As a personal note of contrast, maple root has been used for details such as the cylindrical columns in the living rooms, around the fireplace and on one or two details of the matching furniture.

The furniture was carefully chosen and was designed by Top-House, an interior design shop which has grown from the Ameller and Prats partnership. The sofas are

The structure adapts intelligently to the topography of the site.

The south facade is made entirely of glass and connects with the surroundings. An external terrace follows the profile of the dwelling.

The dining room furniture is palm root, and wood has also been used in the construction of the room's cylindrical columns.

The central tables match the Carrara marble chimney in a bright space with glass facings.

leather-upholstered in colours which blend with the decor of each area. The centre tables match the marble fireplace. The dining room fireplace, armchairs and sideboard are in an exclusive palmroot design. Special attention has been paid to the bathrooms. The master bathroom, which forms part of the bedroom suite, is in Arabescato marble and the walls decorated in Venetian paint. One of the other three bathrooms is also decorated in the same paint and has a glass dresser top with a stainless steel basin that contrasts with the other two more conventionally styled sanitary units. Finally, the furniture in the kitchen is in white Siematic with stainless steel fittings and grey stone flooring. Each bedroom has been given a personal touch by using different counterpanes on the beds.

The kitchen furniture is white Siematic with a stainless steel finish, on grey stoneware floor tiling. Some walls feature pearl-grey granite.

Interior view of one of the bathrooms.

Bathroom with glass-topped surfaces, stainless steel sink and blue facings contrasting with other more formal facings.

Joan Maria Pascual and his P/S/P studio, in partnership with the interior designers Ernest Ameller and Xavier Prats, have succeeded in creating a comfortable home equipped with the most modern conveniences which is a splendid example of good taste and exquisite decor. The design has channelled the possibilities of the vast amounts of light and the privileged situation which the house enjoys, turning it into an unusual and ideal space at any time of year.

The bathroom of the main bedroom is executed in Arabescato marble.

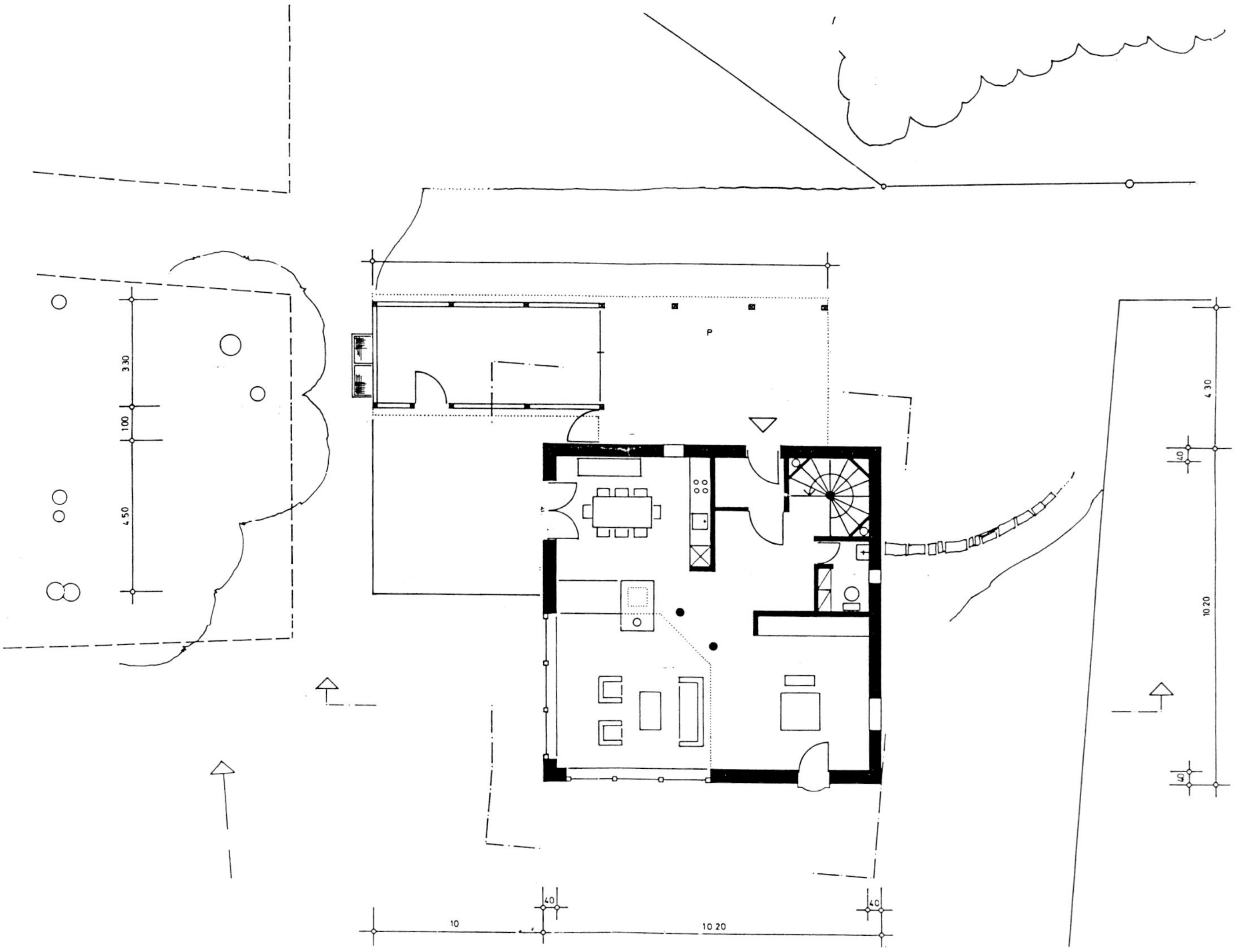
P
3.30
1.00
4.50
4.30
40
10.20
40
40
10
10.20
40

Ground plan of the property.

Large pictures windows in a cubic house

Hans-Jorg Ruch & Urs Husler

This is a rather special house, in Saint Moritz in the upper Engadine valley, where the jet set gather and where winter sports are at the centre of everything. But there is another less well-known side to this world too, that of mountain traditions and the people who live here all year round.

One such person is the architect Hans-Jorg Ruch who built this house for his own family deep in the woods which surround the lake. It's not far from the Hotel-Restaurant Meierei, a popular destination for horse-drawn sleighs, cross-country skiers, walkers and lovers of good regional cooking.

The base of the house is square, predetermined by the edge of the woods on the one hand and the boundary of the next-door property on the other. The architect placed two immense windows on the corner of the house facing the lake, opening the interior diagonally onto a wonderful view of lake and mountain.

Hans-Jorg Ruch, who was born in 1946 in Bellach, Switzerland, studied architecture in the Federal Institute of Technology (ETH) in Zurich. He travelled extensively in order to become familiar with as wide a range of architectural forms as possible before joining Husler to set up a practice in St. Moritz. Amongst his most prominent works are: the new gallery for the Thyssen-Bornemizsa collection in Lugano; the County Art Gallery in Coira (Switzerland), which he designed with two other architects; the house and workplace of the engineer Walter Bieler in Bonaduz; and a studio for gallery owner Bruno Bischofberger in St. Moritz.

View across the living room, taken from one of the picture windows.

One corner of the living room, showing the well-lit kitchen on the left.

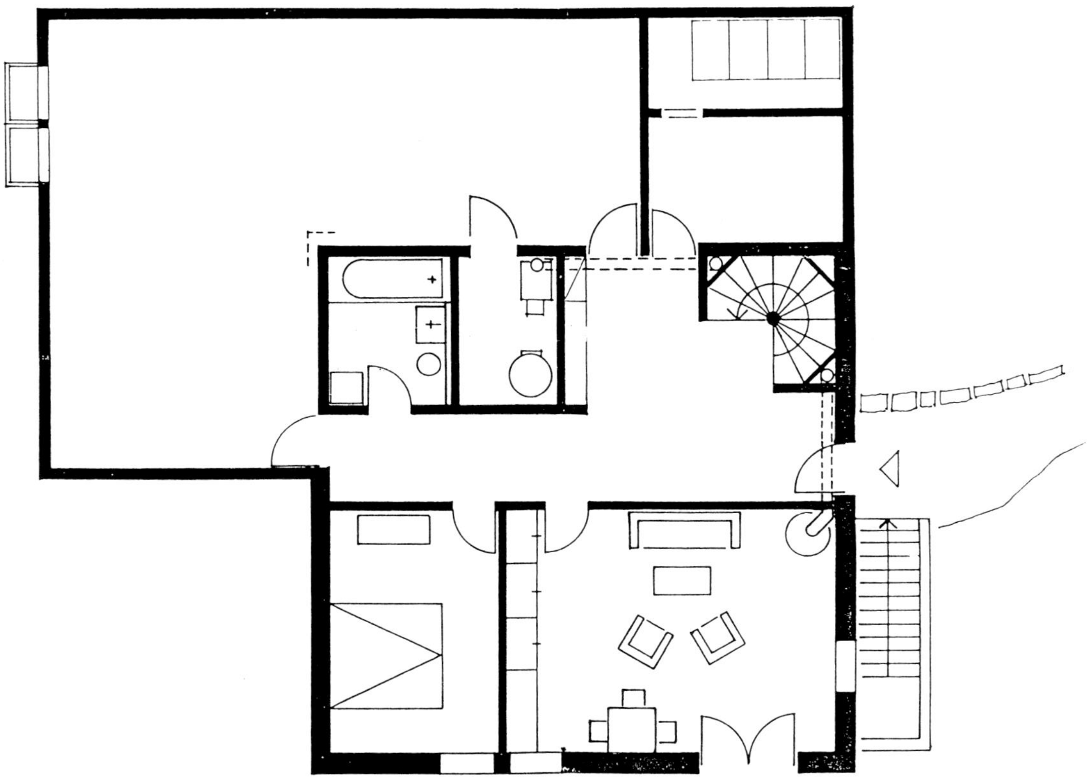

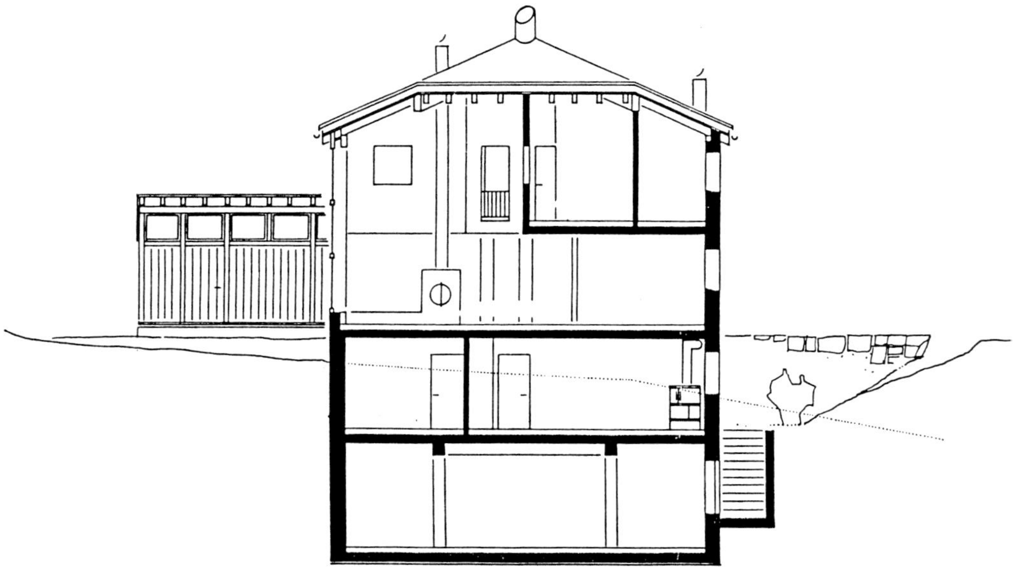

Plan of the entrance floor.

Section of the house and garage.

Detail of the corner where the large windows meet.

The living room seen from above: the sofa, rug, hearth and chimney.

View of the interior, showing the fireplace in the centre of the room.

Urs Husler was born in Zurich in 1945 and studied architecture there. He has worked with several architects including Peter Lorenz and Ruch and has contributed to various publications. Amongst his most noteworthy works are the plans and execution of the Marti Zumikon single-family dwelling in Eglisau; several houses in the Engadine; and the plan of the Egger house, also in Eglisau.

Because of the climate, it is important to find practical, basic ways to solve technical problems. "The house must be like a rock, a stone. The setting and nature play a fundamental role here and the house must be in harmony with these elements, fruit of its own vital energy," *say the architects.*

The way this house is built is extremely clean-cut, essentially geometrical and robust. The main problem was how to connect the house to the surroundings, which is why the vast window panels splitting two sides of the square from floor to roof are so important. The open angle formed by these window panels becomes an interior patio, a link between the house and the woods, a way of bringing the sky and the lake into people's lives.

The materials used reflect the philosophy on which the design of the house is based. The walls are painted in non-synthetic white and grey paints. The natural colours change in tone according to the intensity of the light.

The window are double-glazed because the climate calls for resilient materials which can resist strong winds and heavy snowfalls. (The roof of a house in the mountainous parts of this region must be able to withstand a weight of 1000 kg per square metre.) The

Plan of the top floor.

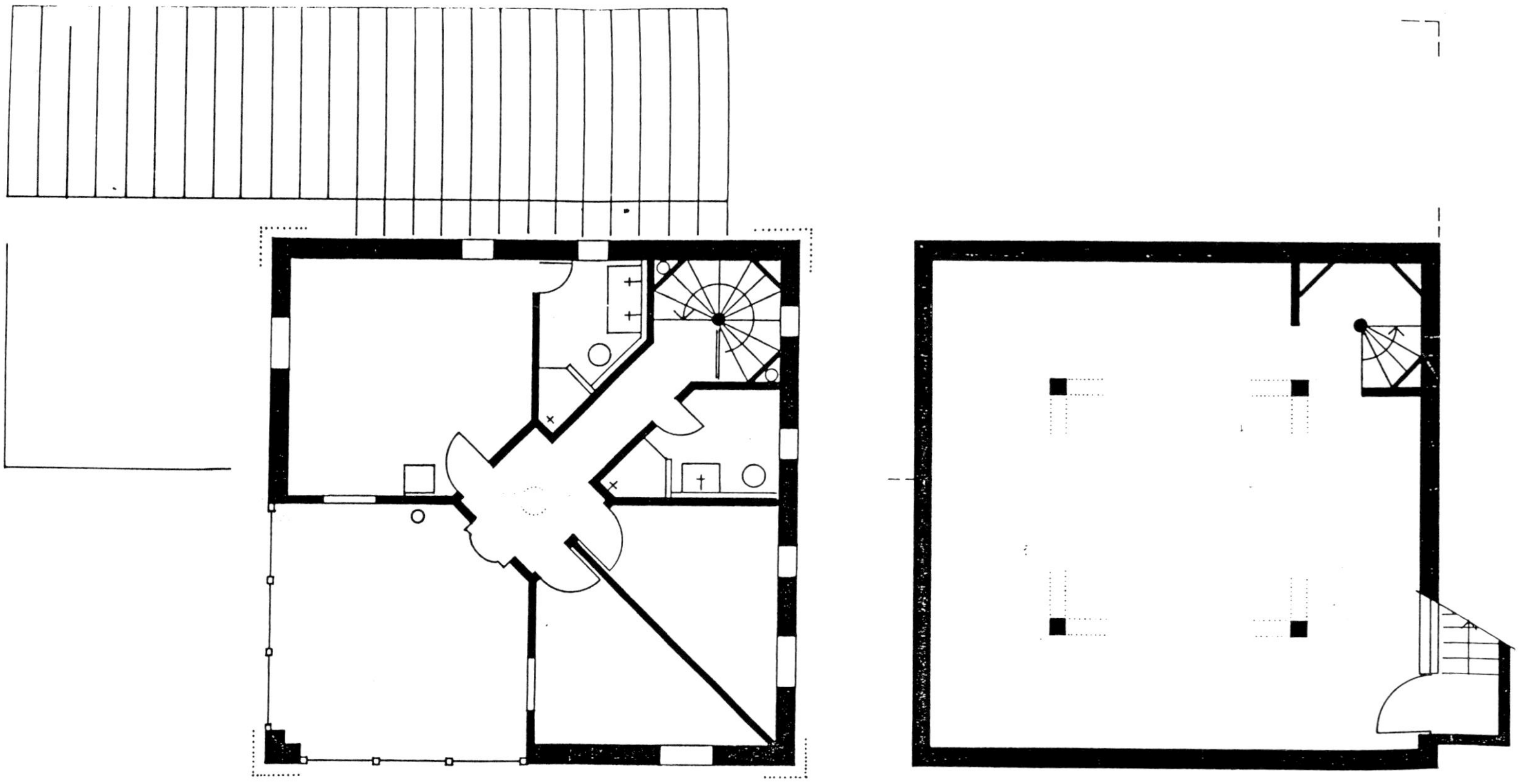

pine beams of the roof frame are slender in order to maintain the harmony between the interior and exterior world.

The garage is a wooden structure quite separate from the house which forms a totally independent unit.

The outside walls of the house are in strong contrast to each other: the rear ones are closed and compact while the front ones with their big windows open out on to the landscape, woods, lakes and sun, allowing anyone to see into the house from outside.

The window panels, which are the focal point of the interior of the house, give the illusion of a house within a house, an idea which is further accentuated by the use of inside windows which open from the bedrooms onto the living space, and through the window panels to the lake.

The small balcony at the end of the first-floor corridor running diagonally across the square of the house reinforces this notion. The living space is so organised that the diagonals that link the opposite corners of the square are unbroken, thus creating a very open, airy space. The height of each living area is also calculated with respect to the sun, which enters the house at all angles at least once a day. Natural considerations and questions of energy saving are not forgotten in this house either. The house is heated by the window panels and by a stove installed between the living area and the kitchen, just as if it were a little house within a house. True to local custom, there is a trap door above the stove which opens up in the floor of the bedroom, thus efficiently spreading the heat to the upper floor. The oil-fired central

Partial view of the living room from the upper level, showing one of the picture windows.

Detail showing the pilars in the dining room and the stairs to the upper level.

heating system built into the flooring is seldom used.

The shape of the house dominates family life. You can see the living area from the bedrooms and you can keep an eye on all parts of the house from the kitchen, including the wooden veranda outside. This is much used during the summer months because it is sheltered from the wind and catches the sun all day long thanks to the glass facades. Most of the furniture in the house is antique, bought by the architect and restored so that it retains its original features. One example is the bed in the master bedroom which bears the date 1605. In the children's bedrooms there are quaint little beds and many wooden toys, modern replicas of traditional toys of the region. There is also a pencil drawing of a human figure by Lukas Roner in the hall. Mixed in with these are modern, Bauhaus-style elements: Mies van der Rohe chairs in the dining room; Marcel Breuer chairs in the sitting room. The sofa, by Gae Aulenti, is the Stringa de la Poltronovo design. The carpets were bought on trips to Africa and South America. Over the display unit in the dining area is a painting by artist and jazz musician Lukas Roner. The display unit, from an old bakery in Pontresina, contains a collection of locks bought during trips to India, Nepal and Morocco. Also in the dining area are three wooden sculptures by Schang Hutter and, at the other end of the bench, three house-shaped wooden pieces by the architect himself. The puppet on the wall is from Burma and the piece of sculpture next to the columns comes from Kenya. The tree-sculpture in the corner between the two window panels is by the Italian sculptor

The balcony at the end of the first-floor corridor is one of several elements reinforcing internal communication.

The children's room.

Ferdinando Codognoto and, on the balcony, the archaic-looking iron sleigh is by the Swiss sculptor Kurt Sigrist.

The sitting room floor is paved with grey tiles by Rignano Sull'Arno. The columns are made of the same material as the ventilation pipes, filled with cement and varnished, and the wood used is the most ordinary: pine.

Lighting is provided by small, recessed lamps which do not distract from the open design of the hallway. The lamp on the dining room table is one of the many finds from the demolition of old hotels in St. Moritz. The locks, sanitary fixtures and taps came from the same source. The lighting on the stairs and the small interior balcony was designed by Charles Keller. The standard lamp in the sitting room is by Oluce, Italy, and the one on the kitchen table is another find: an old street lamp from Zurich.

There are many plants all through the house, some of which come from South America, and they provide original splashes of green.

The originality of this house in St. Moritz designed by Ruch and Husler lies in the use of big window panels which define the house both inside and out: outside as a cube and inside with its sunny open spaces and a style of decoration which mixes restored antiques with more modern elements, giving the house indisputable personality and beauty.

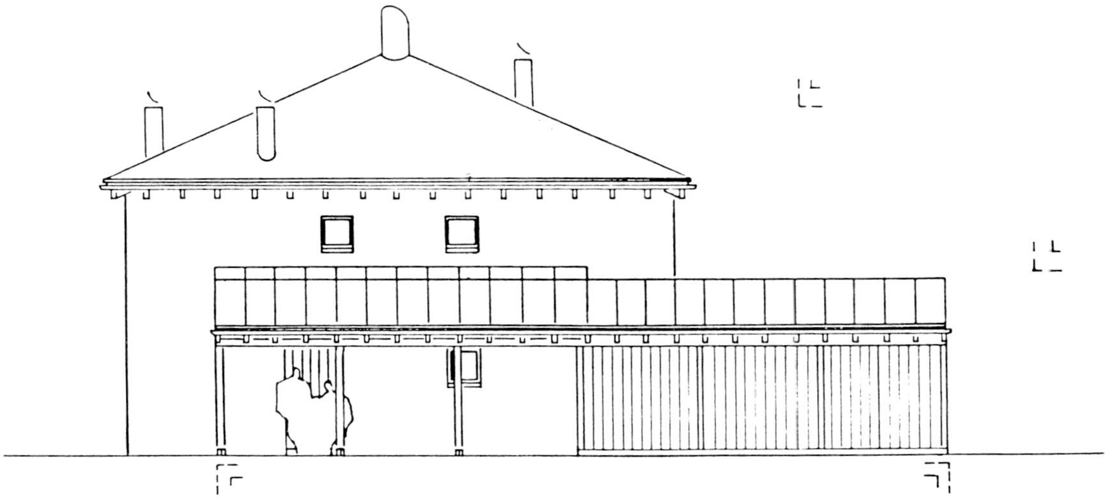

Elevations of the clearly contrasting front and back of the house.

.Elevation of the side of the house, showing the slope down to the lake.

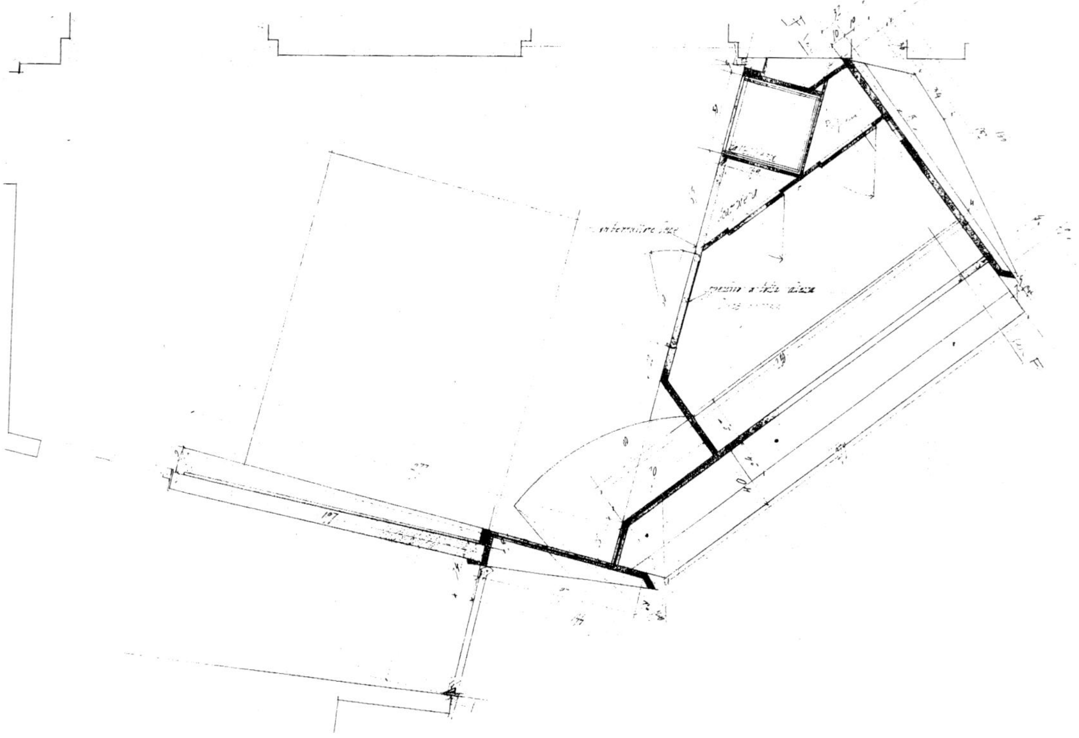

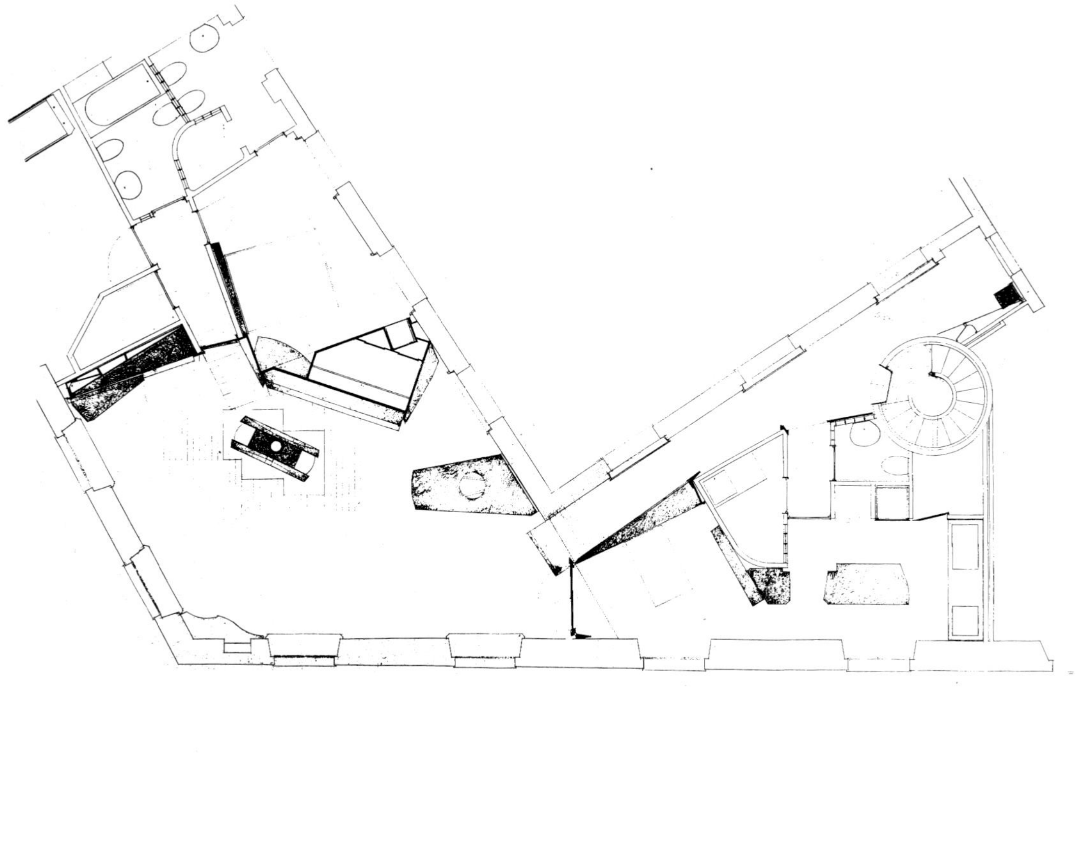

Plan of the upper floor.

Plan of the main level.

Insinga House

Umberto Riva

Umberto Riva was born in Milan in 1928, received his degree in Venice in 1959, and was enrolled in the Milan professional Register of Engineers and Architects in 1960. In addition to the planning of family houses (Stintino House in Sardinia with Drugman, for which they won the 1964 INARCH regional award, the Oliveto Lario House with Scarpini, Taino and Osmate and other residences in Milan), bars, restaurants and office and apartment interiors, Riva has also devoted much of his career to the design of numerous products (chiefly lights and tables) in the fields of decorative and industrial arts.

Umberto Riva demonstrates through this interior organisation of an existing structure on the Via Arena in Milan the exceptional power of his creative style. This is a brilliant exercise in the interpretation of the physical characteristics of an apartment whose only expressive element is the disposition of openings. In taking on this project, Riva did not hesitate to explore architectural theories on the renovation process and arrived at the conclusion that, in such an awkward setting, the most reasonable solution was to ignore all of the current stereotypes and create a language that would offer a personal approach to the rehabilitation process.

In this case, his fundamental break with convention consisted in granting one of the most frequently neglected areas of a residence – the corridor – the key function of the living space. The interior was designed with an eye to movement, and a natural circulation pattern was established based on the free-flowing sequences and perspectives that determine its dynamic

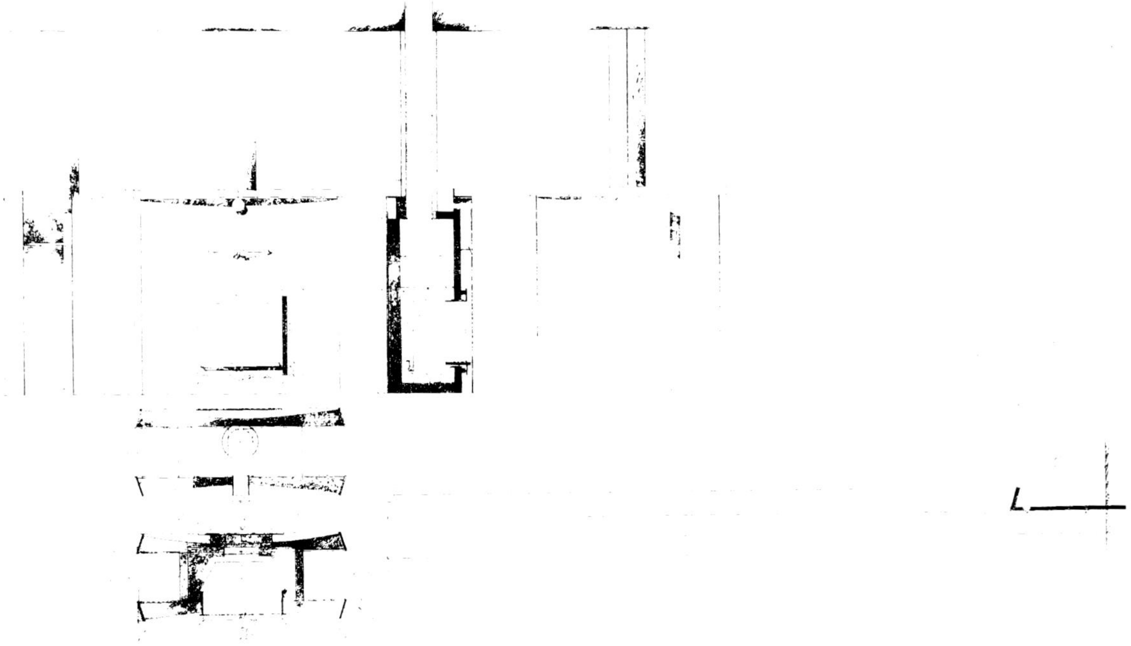

Sketches for the dining table, specially designed to make the most of the awkward space available.

Various sections of the fireplace and flue.

The entrance hall and corridor, with a coatrack and the bulge of the spiral staircase on the left.

Main door and entrance hall, featuring the coatrack-cum-umbrella stand.

The furnishings are comfortable, modern and aesthetically warm.

The modern line of the umbrella stand by the main door sets the tone.

image. To achieve this, there are no obstacles or physical boundaries, the distribution being defined by non-structural elements (the table, the fireplace and the flooring). These components now serve an additional function in indicating the internal itinerary. The various rooms are either articulated by this route or integrated with it, and provided with spaciousness and light.

Riva's singular insight is reflected in the domination of the non-architectural components of the distribution system. However, the intrinsic nature of the existing space required a bold and unusual plan, so that the individual style of the planner is obscured by the complex demands of the intervention. This corner apartment has two open facades with an unequal number of windows: seven face the courtyard and eight face the street, with several of these overlooking the gardens.

This regular placement of the openings is the most expressive motif of the apartment, and the layout takes the utmost advantage of the transparency they offer. The usable living area consisted of two intersecting trapezia with differences in both the orientation and in the size of their smaller sides, which resulted in wasted space and angular corners that were difficult to use. Another determining aspect of this highly irregular floor plan was the location of the entrance in one of the corners of the smaller trapezoidal space. On the positive side, the apartment has a magnificent terrace that overlooks the courtyard.

With these inconvenient volumetric characteristics as the point of departure, the Milanese architect introduced

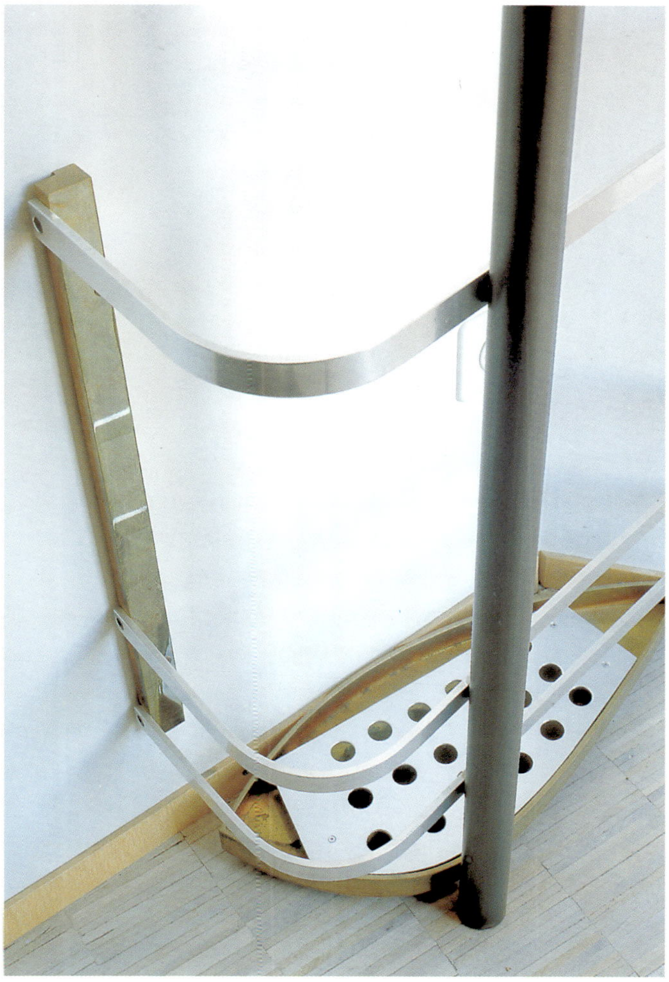

a domestic programme which made it eminently livable. The physical aspects called for an out-of-the-ordinary layout, based on two key concepts that distance this intervention from the mainstream. Firstly, no architectural conventions were employed in the design beyond the most basic functional elements, and these were adapted to the specific nature of the existing volume. Secondly, he did not impose his own individuality on the space and its programme.

A conventional articulation of the functional programme could not be carried out in such an irregular volume. The architect had to ignore those formulas that emphasised the importance of isolated, independent rooms. For an apartment governed by straight lines and angles that continually changed direction, Riva chose to grant special significance to the corridor. Thus he designed a logical circulation pattern that begins at the entrance and, running parallel to the partition wall of the smaller trapezium, leads to the terrace connected to the large living room.

The concept of movement is dramatised by this natural circulation route that offers the apartment a continuity of perspective. In this way, it is impossible to view the space as a static, unitary and complete area that does not respond in any sense to the volumetric features of the premises. The visual reading is based on the corridor, which has been transformed into a series of richly expressive sequences, of partial views and scattered fragments that are drawn into a unity by the material treatment, the use of colour and the natural light, and by its harmonious atmosphere.

In the generous living room formed by this simple arrangement, the continuity of the perspectives and of the circulation route has been achieved through pieces of furniture and other non-structural items. The most impressive are the table and the fireplace, which not only fulfil their customary functions, but also suggest the route to the bedrooms. The table expresses the transition between the entrance hallway and the living room through a positioning that indicates the change in direction. It is a panel whose extension section appears to be built into the wall, giving a visual impression of strength. In this way, a movable component is transformed into a fixed element that, in spite of its seeming fragility, lends solidity to the interior route. The

.View across the living room, with the dining area and kitchen in the background.

General view of the living room, dominated by the huge freestanding fireplace.

The rear of the fireplace, showing the chromatically differentiated recessed sides.

oculus window in the centre, (through which the control mechanism of the extension can be seen) and the texture of the wood complete the design of this table.

The prefabricated fireplace, on the other hand, appears as a free-standing solid rectangular mass in two parallel sections executed in two different colours and topped by a cylindrical chimney flue. Its placement creates a small rear passageway that provides access to the more private areas. In addition to the table and the fireplace, other articulating elements distributed throughout the interior help to define its volume. Among them are the metal coat rack in the entryway, the change of direction in the pattern of the wood flooring, and the plaster moulding of the ceiling.

The interior plate glass window allows the corridor to be lit naturally through the kitchen.

The living room is closed off by a large dresser at its far end.

Wood is used throughout to great effect, including for the bookshelves.

The dining area; the approach to the decoration was to use warm yet light tones.

View across the lower floor from the kitchen to one of the living-room windows.

The initial project also included the development of the terrace above, but up to the present time, only the communication system has been completed. The curved section of the partition at the beginning of the corridor repeats the cylindrical development of the stairway, with its inner surface faced in brick and the sumptuous plastic form of the steps. Another of the dominant aspects of the apartment is the attention focused on the openings, on the views of the urban setting and on the transparency of the interior. The spacious, luminous interior atmosphere is emphasized by the use of wooden furniture, an honest, warm material that is well-suited to the creative work of the Milanese architect.

In short, Umberto Riva's intervention in this apartment on the Via Arena in Milan is a magnificent exercise in spatial distribution, with an economy of expression that seeks to reorder a ground plan that was inconvenient as it was attractive. To accomplish this, he had to look beyond the more conventional models of residential works and grant a leading role to one of the least significant elements of the programme, the corridor. By this means, the appearance is no longer static and unitary, but rather a rich series of visual sequences and fragments, governed by the idea of movement. Instead of partition walls, the internal programme is articulated by more unusual components. Regarding the work as a whole, the architect has successfully achieved his objectives, which implied foregoing the pretensions of the 'artist/architect', although the interior mood is imbued with his unique creative vision.

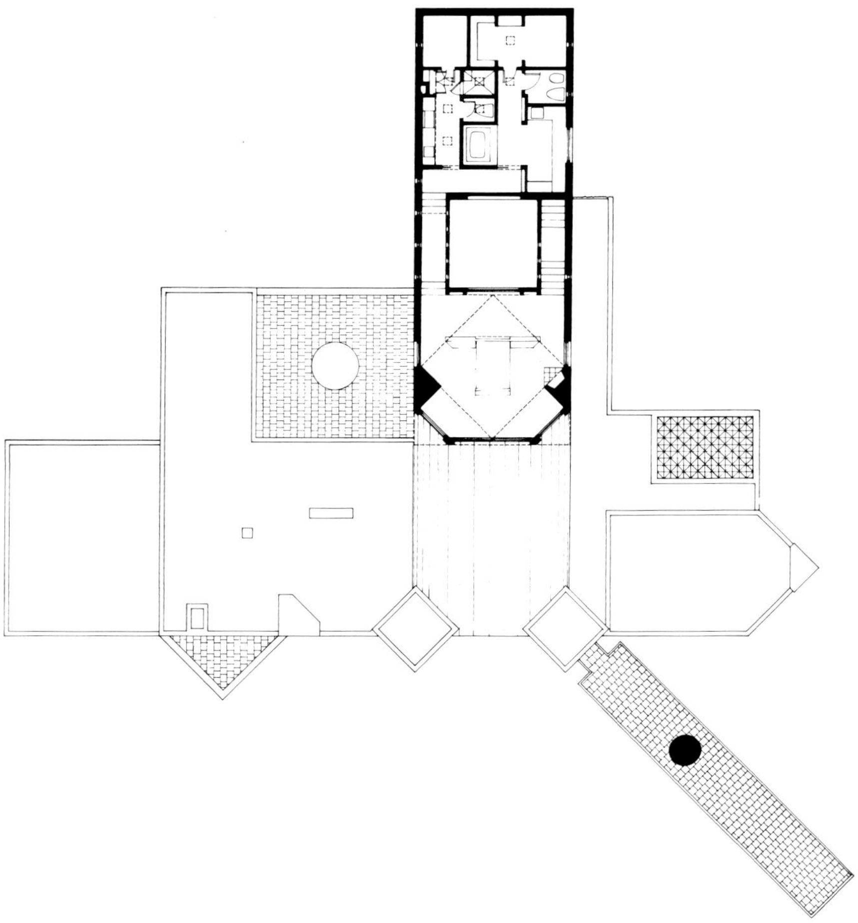

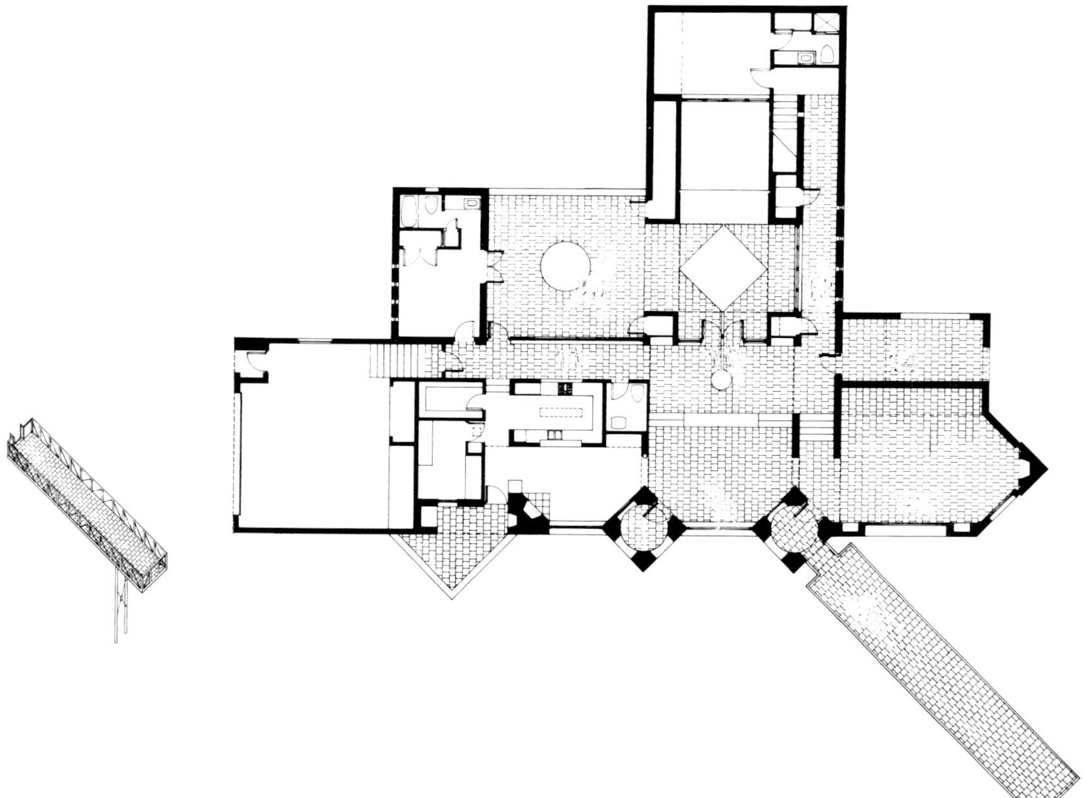

Plan of the upper floor.

Plan of the ground floor and axonometric representation of the bridge.

An incomplete bridge as a vehicle of communication

Antoine Predock

The future owners of this single-family dwelling designed by Antoine Predock wanted to translate their interest in the arts to a home spiritually linked to the desert where it was to be sited and which, in turn, would be an ideal setting for exhibiting their valuable collections. The temple also had to provide accommodation for small and large groups of guests, and had to feature an independent and private attic for the exclusive use of the owners.

Located on the side of a mountain, this single-family dwelling was constructed in Paradise Valley in the middle of the Arizona desert in the United States. The pronounced unevenness of the irregular and sheer terrain, as well as its positioning, were the principal factors determining the building. At the same time, its structure and layout guarantee a beautiful view of the valley below and the towns extending as far as the horizon. The site takes up approximately one acre.

Antoine Predock studied at the University of New Mexico and Columbia University, graduating in architecture in 1962. He set up his own practice in 1967, and since then has dedicated himself exclusively to this profession.

In addition to his professional activities, it is worth mentioning his work as a teacher, since he has been guest lecturer and critic at leading American universities – Arizona State University, Harvard University, the Southern California Institute of Architecture and UCLA. In 1981 he was co-opted onto the management board of the National Design Committee of the American Institute

The swimming pool, leading to the living room, and above these, the master bedroom.

The corridor provides an intermediate space between the house and the exterior.

Axonometric view of the house.

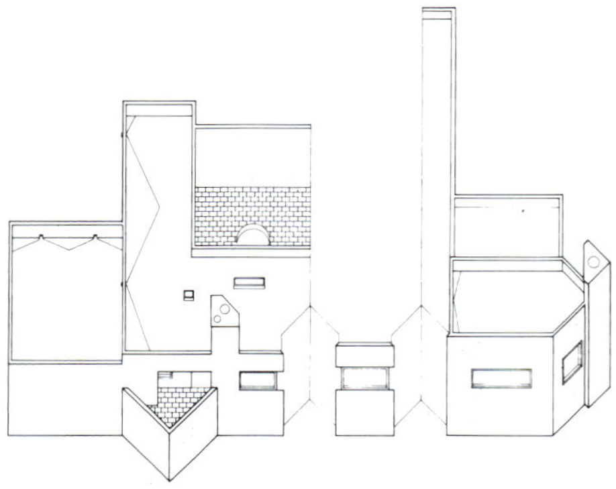

of Architects (AIA). His architectural projects are numerous and span Arizona, California, Colorado, New Mexico, Nevada, Wyoming and NCARB. He has also undertaken landscaping work in New Mexico. A member of the American Institute of Architects and of the American Academy in Rome, he has received a large number of prizes and citations; he is known worldwide for his exhibitions and lectures, and as the author of numerous articles published in specialist journals.

This architectural project was planned in 1986 and executed in the course of 1989. Mitzi Vernon and Judy Zuber were responsible for the interior design.

The residence consists of two clearly differentiated and independent levels on a completely irregular ground plan. The ground or access floor, which is the main body of the building, includes a large sitting room which connects, successively, with the dining room and a breakfast area next to the kitchen. An incomplete bridge (a decisively unusual construction from the external aspect of the building) following a diagonal line begins in an intermediate area next to the sitting room. Behind these rooms is the gallery where the works of art are exhibited, which also cover the walls of a long connecting corridor leading to the garage at the opposite end of the house. At the back of the house, opening onto an interior patio with a rhombus-shaped pond, is a guest bedroom with bathroom. Finally, a ramp leads to the studio. Next to this a staircase leads to the top floor.

The attic on this floor is much smaller, and its ground plan perfectly rectangular. This level contains the master

View across the spacious, irregularly shaped living room with its multiple vistas.

bedroom, an enormous bathroom-cum-dressing room, a swimming pool and a terrace, which looks out over the horizon and offers splendid view. Both levels are connected by open spaces.

By using a studied juxtaposition of the two main bodies, the architect has achieved dynamic equilibrium in this single-family dwelling. The volume, which runs from north to south as an annex to the divided blocks, links the building to the mountainside. Inside, a freshwater spring forms a waterfall which flows into a silent swimming pool, and subsequently into a circular section located at the entrance to the gallery.

Above the water looms the solitary attic with the master bedroom, which has two contrasting functions: a private and interior space which is also the control tower. The views, framed by the top-floor windows, overlook the swimming pool and gallery and, externally, facing Camelback Mountain, Scoosdale and Phoenix, they intensify this duality. This main room is crowned by two observation towers which form the southern wall of the dining room gallery.

The house lies on an east-west axis, contrary to which there is stuccoed work room supported by the arms of the tower which jut out from the other block, incorporating the more public household rooms.

The bridge, positioned diagonally, serves as a frame for the entrance portico for potential visitors and has a platform with excellent views next to the sitting room. The French limestone repeated in the sitting room and on the floor of this unfinished balcony has a charming feel to it,

View through the living room to the swimming pool and other rooms beyond.

extremely difficult to attain in architecture. A clear view of the seasonal and daily changes occurring on the Phoenix horizon, and an uninterrupted view from the master bedroom, are both a result of the strategic construction of this bridge. Inaccessible as it seems, this architectural feature which appears to go nowhere becomes a vehicle transporting the occupants to the various areas.

The greyish colour of the concrete walls, combined with the earth-coloured brickwork of the towers, establishes a spontaneous link between the building and the landscape.

The structure of the building consists of a series of concrete blocks, connecting and retaining walls, and a wooden ceiling and floor. As far as materials are concerned, the masonry is principally bare sandbased

At one end of the living room a picture window affords a fine view of the valley.

The interior is intimately linked to the exterior throughout the construction.

concrete, stucco, French limestone covering the steel floor, subsequently faced with deciduous hardwood, and plaster walls and ceilings finished in black granite.

The owner's love of art, together with their explicit desire to relate it to the desert and its peculiar spirit, gave Antoine Predock the idea of duality for this unique single-family dwelling.

The oblique and incomplete bridge as the starting and finishing points of the building, becomes a fundamental and defining element which ratifies its continuously contradictory character, a peculiarity endowing it with a multitude of functions, differentiating it from its uniform environment and projecting it, by means of certain geometric parameters, towards the endless horizon.

Connecting windows and paving-type floor tiles enhance the relationship between interior and exterior.

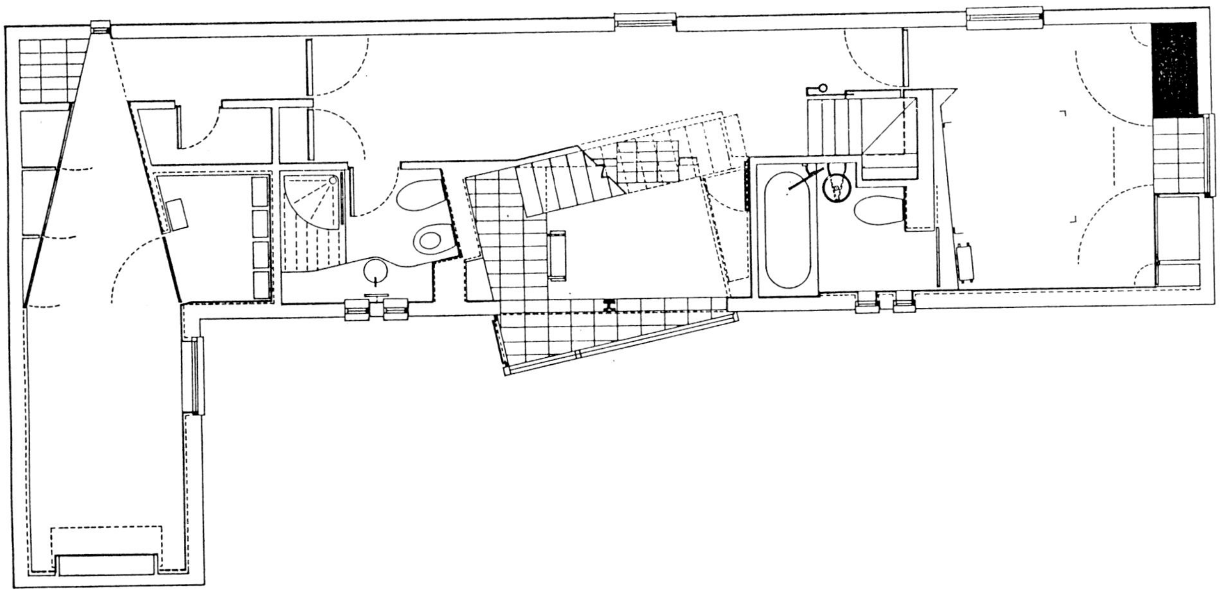

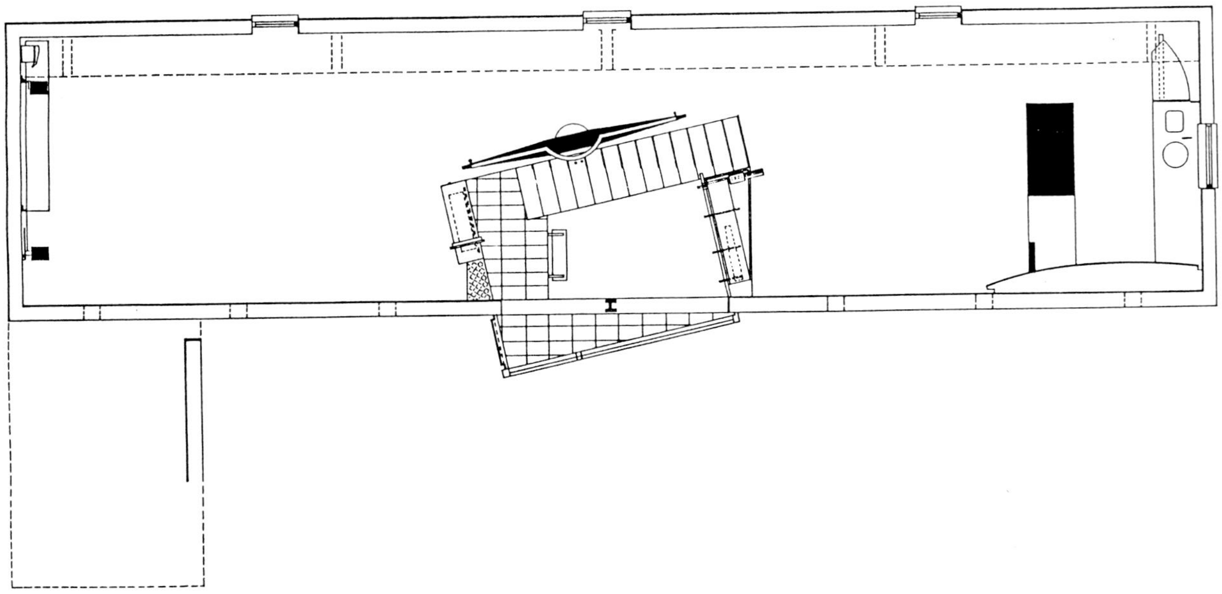

Plans of the ground and upper floors respectively.

Blackburn House

Architekturbüro Bolles-Wilson

Peter L. Wilson, born in Melbourne, Australia, in 1950, trained at the University of Melbourne from 1968 to 1972 and continued his studies at the Architectural Association of London, graduating in 1974. He taught there from 1978 until 1988. In 1980 in London he founded the Wilson Partnership studio, which became the Architekturbüro Bolles-Wilson seven years later, with offices in London and Münster.

Julia B. Bolles-Wilson was born in Münster, studied at the University of Karlsruhe from 1968 to 1976, underwent postgraduate training at the Architectural Association of London (1977-78), and subsequently joined the two above architecture studios.

Eberhard Kleffner, born in Ostbevern, Germany, also studied at the University of Karlsruhe. In 1988 he joined the Architekturbüro Bolles-Wilson.

The following are their major joint projects: Water House in 1976 (Shenkenshinku third prize); the Hamburg Domplatz competition, which they won in 1984; the Münster City Museum and Library (first prize, 1985); Blackburn House in London and the second floor of the Münster Library, the urban plan of the city of Rotterdam, a child-care centre in Frankfurt and the Krakow Urban Villa (Shenkenshiku third prize), all in 1988; the Cosmos Street Office Building in Tokyo, the Church Meeting House in Münster, the Karlsruhe Art + Media Museum (second prize) and the Asperen Fort Bridge (1989); the Folly Exposition in Osaka, the Münster Technology Hof, Yellow (a furniture store and showroom in Münster) and a private house in Tokyo (1990).

One corner of the ground floor is used as a study.

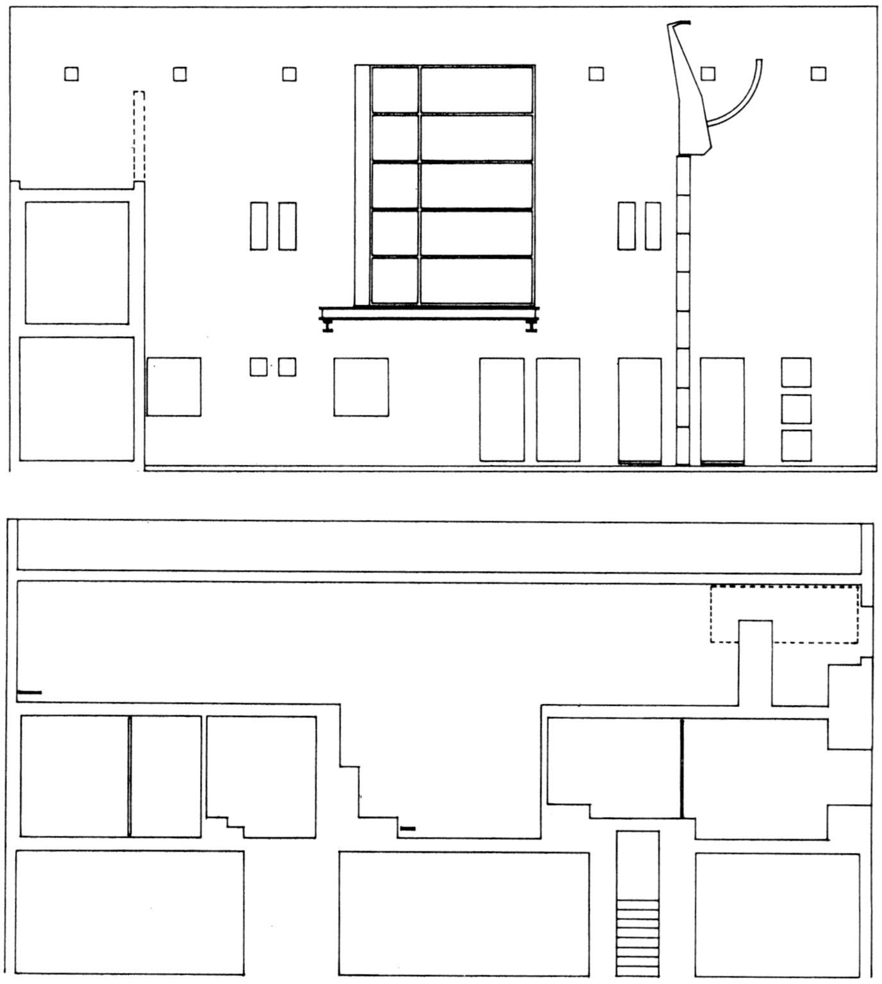

Lateral cross section and cross section.

Blackburn House represents the triumph of tenacity over the frustrating limitations on creative, revolutionary construction in England and, more specifically, in an urban setting such as London. Thanks to the understanding of openminded clients and to favourable planning conditions, the studio formed by Peter Wilson, Julia Bolles-Wilson and Eberhard Kleffner successfully completed an exceptional work whose siting on the streets of the British capital would have been difficult. The structure is an expressive and plastic architectural exercise and, at the same time, a delicate and subtle interior design.

The architects remodelled several old structures of scant aesthetic value, adding a new volumetry that departed in both form and function from the original buildings. According to Wilson himself, the project represents a rejection of the established canons, serving as a pause, an interruption in the urban context of contemporary society. To achieve this end the building was envisioned as an autonomous object, as an independent mass to serve as a point of reference and a link. Without representing an obvious intrusion in the urban setting, this combined office and residence illustrates a profusion of contemporary, inventive ideas, particularly on themes concerning the architectural process and the internal programme.

As mentioned above, the likelihood of constructing a modern, ambitious piece of architecture in present-day London is very remote. Only the open minds of the clients (David and Janice Blackburn) and, most important,

View across the upper floor. Natural light pours in through the plate glass windows of the oblique room and the half concealed skylights that run the length of the building.

The bannister rail not only incorporates a seat but performs a compositional function, punctuating the upper floor.

A corner of the upper floor, with simple bench seating running along the wall.

Geometrical forms predominate in the elements surrounding the stairwell.

the ideal site of the project made its execution possible. However, the relativity of the benefits of the site should be borne in mind, since its only advantage is that it is not visible from the street. This factor allowed the architects complete creative freedom and, with the blessing of the owners, they were able to execute a work that is as unusual as it is attractive.

The intervention involved the restructuring of a group of existing stables that freed a space which had no visual connection with the streets. Within it a new architectural volume could be designed with no typological or legal constraints. The project was planned in accord with Wilson's theories, completely independent from the context, in an attempt to create an isolated structure with its own meaning and values.

The architectural composition was centred exclusively on the two aspects of volume and facade. The first involved completing the original unfinished structure of the stables, at the same time gaining the required space. Regarding the second aspect, much time and energy was devoted to planning the facade in accord with two basic principles. The first was the complete expressive freedom already noted and the second was the shielding of the occupants and the contents from the indifferent visual sequences of the surrounding buildings. With these singular objectives, the conventional sense of the facade was reinterpreted, since the goal in this case was not to show or suggest the interior with respect to the setting, but the opposite: to safeguard and protect that interior.

The angle where the corridor begins to focus inwards; notice the original heating system.

The oblique room and staircase mark the transition between the two levels.

The entrance into the main corridor, complete with umbrella stand.

View of the upper floor from the dining area; straight lines alternate with subtle curves.

Because of its siting, a single facade was planned for the building, and on its surface the entire expressive content of the design would be concentrated. This was determined by the lack of multiple perspectives, a result of its position; only one side of the building is exposed. The basic volume was supplemented by a perpendicular module with a pitched roof, which increased the usable space, screened the main facade from public view and created a small, closed internal street. The entrance to the interior of the building is through this additional structure.

The plasticity of the main elevation is generated by two elements of remarkable fabric, which combine an imaginative aesthetic with utilitarianism. Both provide a compelling contrast to the extreme whiteness of the overall surface and the necessary visual tension in the whole. Secondly, these elements represent attempts to offer practical solutions to the functional problems arising from the indifferent surroundings. The characteristics of these two elements merit a more detailed analysis.

The first is a huge window that emerges halfway up the facade. It extends obliquely across the entire front, initiating an interplay of planes, orientations and convergences that is remarkably effective. The visual effect is reinforced by two external beams that appear to support the projecting structure of the window. The surface is executed in opaque glass (as are the rest of the windows) containing several transparent pieces, and the abstract lines form a subtle link between the interior and the exterior. This blind material was used to shield the house from the unattractive setting, while the stylised transparent sections, in addition to creating a plastic formal pattern, allow the interior to breathe visually. In addition to the protection from the cityscape offered by this facade, a chromatic effect is achieved by the green copper doors on the lower section of the white surface.

The vast window shares the surface of the facade with a second element, partially sculptural, partially architectural, serving both aesthetic and functional purposes. The structure, known as the Totem, is built against the facade and consists of a column executed in welded plastic and stainless steel, an ironic reference to exterior piping that also plays a functional role: to pipe clean water into the house and eject waste. Aesthetically it reinforces the vertical perspective of the building, while

Detail of the bathroom. The coolness of the grey tiling and the metal fittings is offset by the mellow colour of the wood panelling.

The delicately furnished main corridor, showing the protruding steps of the oblique staircase that rises from the adjoining room.

it carries out one of the conventional processes of the domestic programme.

The ground floor accommodates the offices and the two upper storeys constitute the living space. The second major achievement of the project is the interior architecture, a compendium of the most ingenious systems of spatial organisation and interior decor. Each of the blocks is independent, but also interrelated within the overall context of the volumetric configuration, resulting in a single reality of undeniable expressive and conceptual value.

The perpendicular module mentioned above which forms the entrance to the building communicates with the first floor of the residence. This section contains an additional study with converging walls panelled in different types of wood. The rest of the apartment is defined by a longitudinal development on two floors, articulated by an empty space which corresponds in both volume and orientation to the vast oblique window of the facade. All of the rooms are distributed around this interior atrium which links all the perspectives physically and visually.

The first floor contains the more private rooms (the master bedroom, the toilets and the storeroom adjoining the study). This was conceived as a transitional area between the surrounding city and the basic nucleus of the design – the top floor – where the occupants are completely insulated from the urban context. The communications system between these two storeys is a staircase of light, airy design. On the upper level the secluded ambience is related to the exterior only by the transparent fragments in the opaque glass and by a skylight that runs the length of the rear of the roof. Most of the collective household activities take place in this area. There are no structural barriers; the rooms (the living room, the dining room and the communicating kitchen) are ordered on either side of the central space. The back wall is left free for the display of paintings.

The inclusion of the most ambitious designs in furniture and decor constituted a danger to the harmony of the interior. The diversity of artists and styles (Barry Flanagan's hare, Scott Burton's chair, Andy Warhol's portrait, Bruce McLean's and Ron Arad's tables and Jasper Morrison's sofas), and the special attention given to microdesign, could have brought about a fragmentation of the living space. But in spite of the fact that each of these pieces has an autonomous narrative, they are all similar in tone, and disruption was avoided by limiting the selection of materials and by a monochrome treatment. The nature of the decorative elements lies somewhere between architecture and sculpture. This is most apparent in the door furniture, the support column and the projecting platform (all in steel), the vitrine, the stylised table for the high-fidelity system and, most arresting of all, the seat in the central atrium, whose sinuous form seems to float in the interior.

In this project the firm headed by Peter Wilson has executed a masterly combination of exterior and interior architecture from both the conceptual and aesthetic standpoints. Conceptually the work represents a triumph over the rigid, archaic urban building tradition, although to accomplish this the structure had to be concealed from public view. On the facade, all of the most conventional themes have been violated (for example, the glass protects rather that displays) through the use of highly plastic and dramatic elements. In the interior, partitions were rejected in favour of the two-storey open space as the articulator of the rooms. Finally, the iconoclastic designs in decor and furnishings define a way of life and an atmosphere that is completely isolated from the external environment. The concept of the autonomous, independent object governs both the interior and the exterior, safe from any type of constraint the modern city might impose.

Textured metal plate is a recurring feature of the fittings.

Converging walls train the eye towards the slit window, with its glimpse of the exterior.

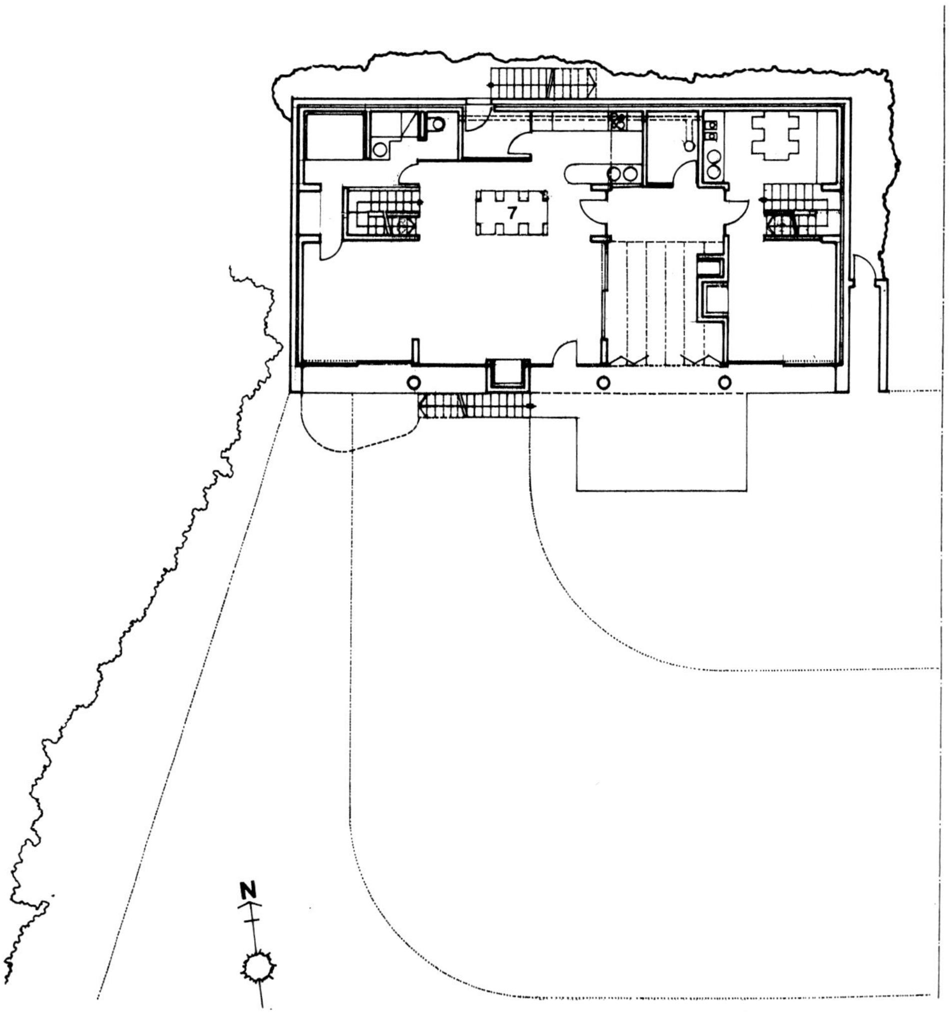
7
N

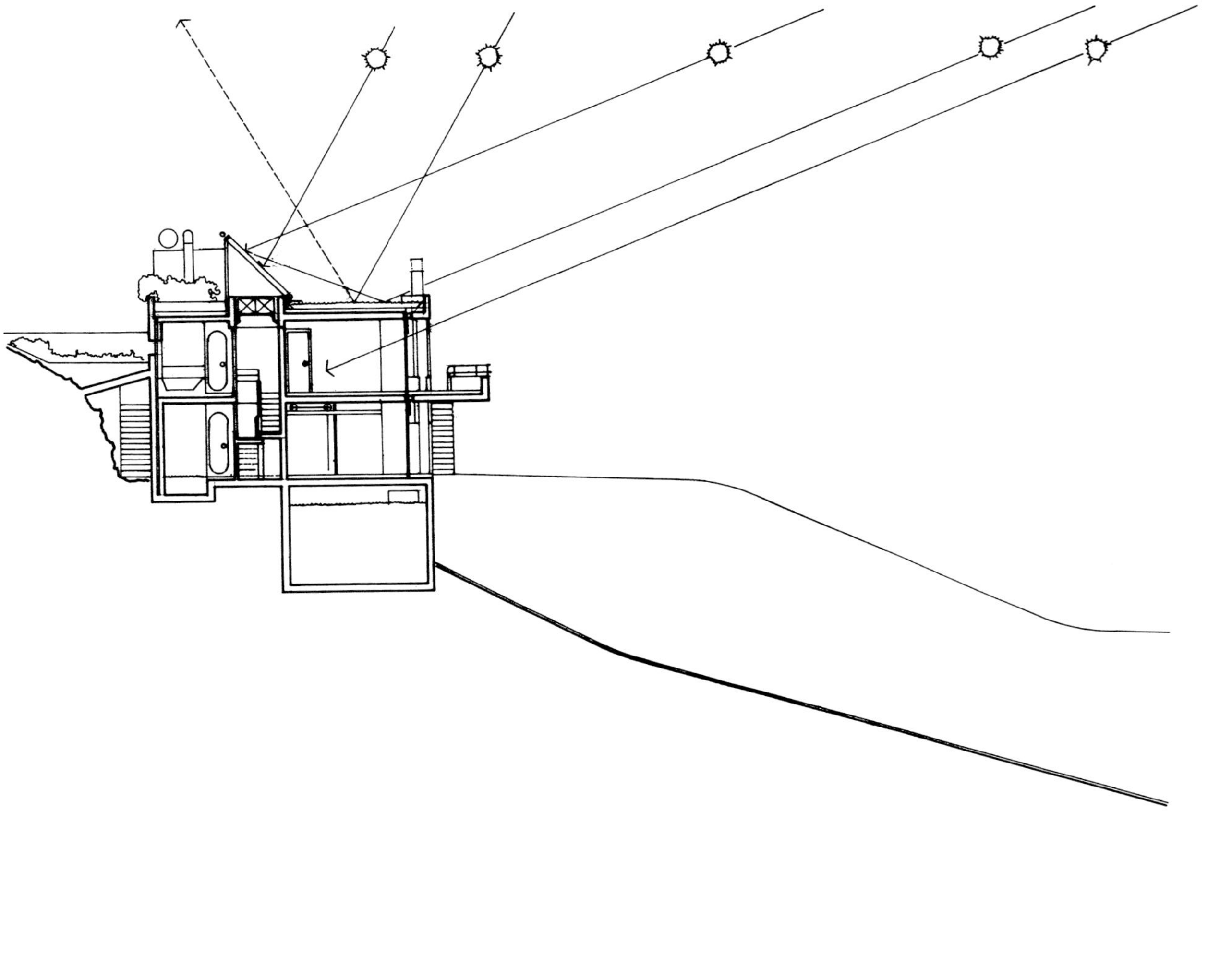

Plan of the middle floor.

Cross section showing the angle of incidence of the sun at different times of day and year.

The symbiosis of nature and technology

Martin Wagner

Built on the top of a hill in the mountainous region of Beredino, this house is surrounded by lush, almost luminous, vegetation. Seen from above, the building, composed of the main house, a winter garden and a guest house, blends unobtrusively into the hillside. Martin Wagner, the architect, called Bigorio House a "sun collecting box", and his description could not be bettered; the sun brings energy, the collector catches it and the box stores it. The house is an excellent example of the use of passive energy, and its technical aspects are a constant theme of debate and discussion.

Martin Wagner was born in 1947 in Baset, where he trained and now works. He completed his training at the Engineering School in Brugg-Windisch and went on to work in Professor D. Schnebli's office in Agno.

He worked in Basel and Paris between 1975 and 1977 where he produced his first independent designs and projects. He later went into practice with Max Wagner in Basel and collaborated with Martin Schmidt in Carona and Fredi Meier in Zurich.

He was an SCI-ARC instructor at the Nîmes, Carona and Vico Morcote Summer Courses, and a guest lecturer at the Swiss Federal Institute of Technology (ETH) in Zurich. At the moment he is in private practice in Carona as well as directing SCI-ARC in Vico Morcote.

This whole building is a contrast between glass, steel and concrete, a strange mixture but each component has a very clear function. The glass, double-glazed and well insulated, is strategically placed so that the natural light will penetrate the house, and at the same time it ensures

The winter garden, used practically all year round, features an open hearth.

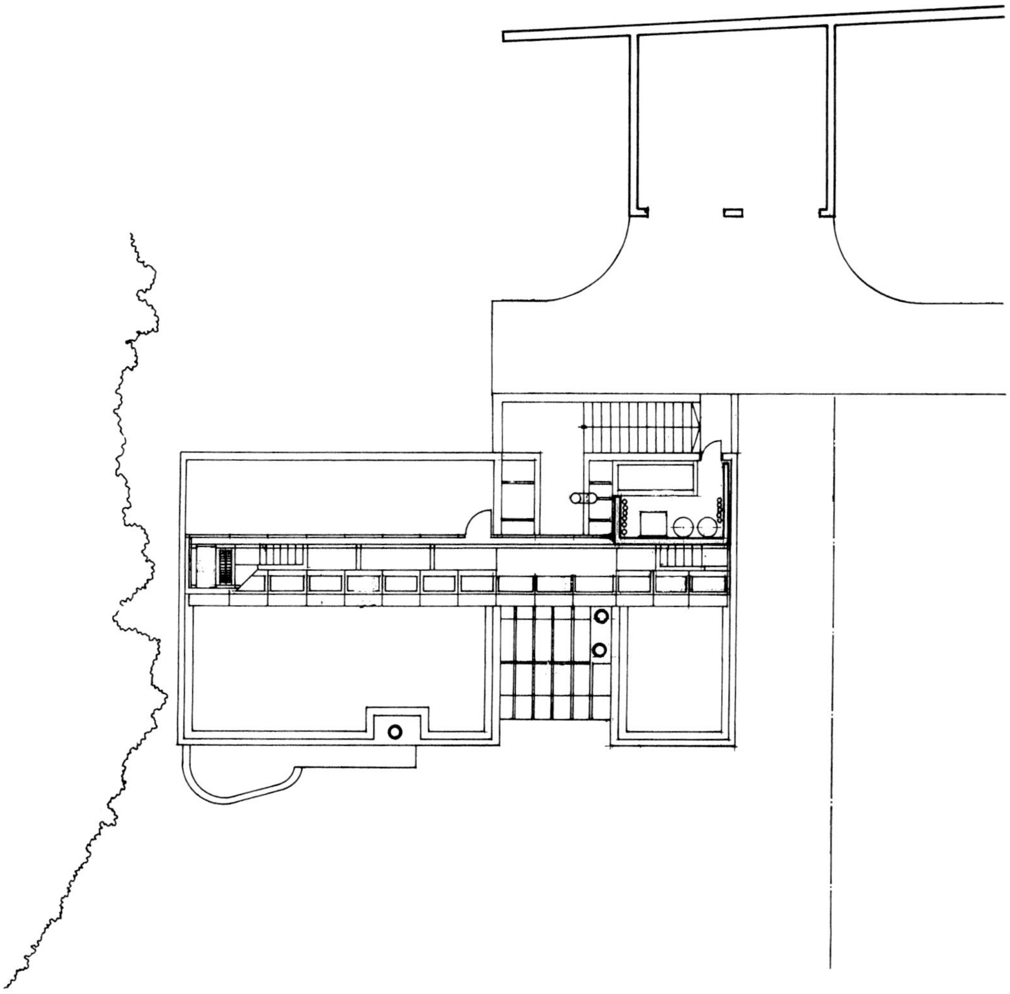

Plan of the lower floor.

close contact with nature. Steel acts as an element of support and union, and concrete is used as a protective casing. Each of these materials has been adapted to serve a specific purpose. The combination is almost a sculpture, highlighted by the cobalt blue window frames and bright red railings. This idea is magically reinforced by the luminous Ticino skies reflected everywhere.

The building is designed as a passive thermal receptor: an insulated glass structure facing southwest. The compact, closed-in shape of the other three sides, the thermal accumulation of the interior masses which radiate the solar heat they have stored, the winter garden which is the link between the house and guest area, and the solar collector on the roof all reinforce this primary aim.

In contrast to the passive role of the solid construction mass, the active elements such as the collectors and energy centre on the roof manage to lighten the overall effect. On sunny days the floor heating takes its heat directly from the collectors. When the weather is overcast a 6 hp thermal pump gets energy from the collectors, air ducts and septic tank and fuels the floor heating through an accumulator. The fireplace also provides extra warmth. It has been proved that when the weather is good, even though outside temperatures are low, an internal temperature of over 20 degrees can be maintained thanks to the energy which is being collected passively throughout the building and actively in the collectors. Although other rational energy houses have been built, the fact is that this house is much admired but rarely emulated; clear proof

The simply furnished living room gives directly onto the verdant Ticino countryside.

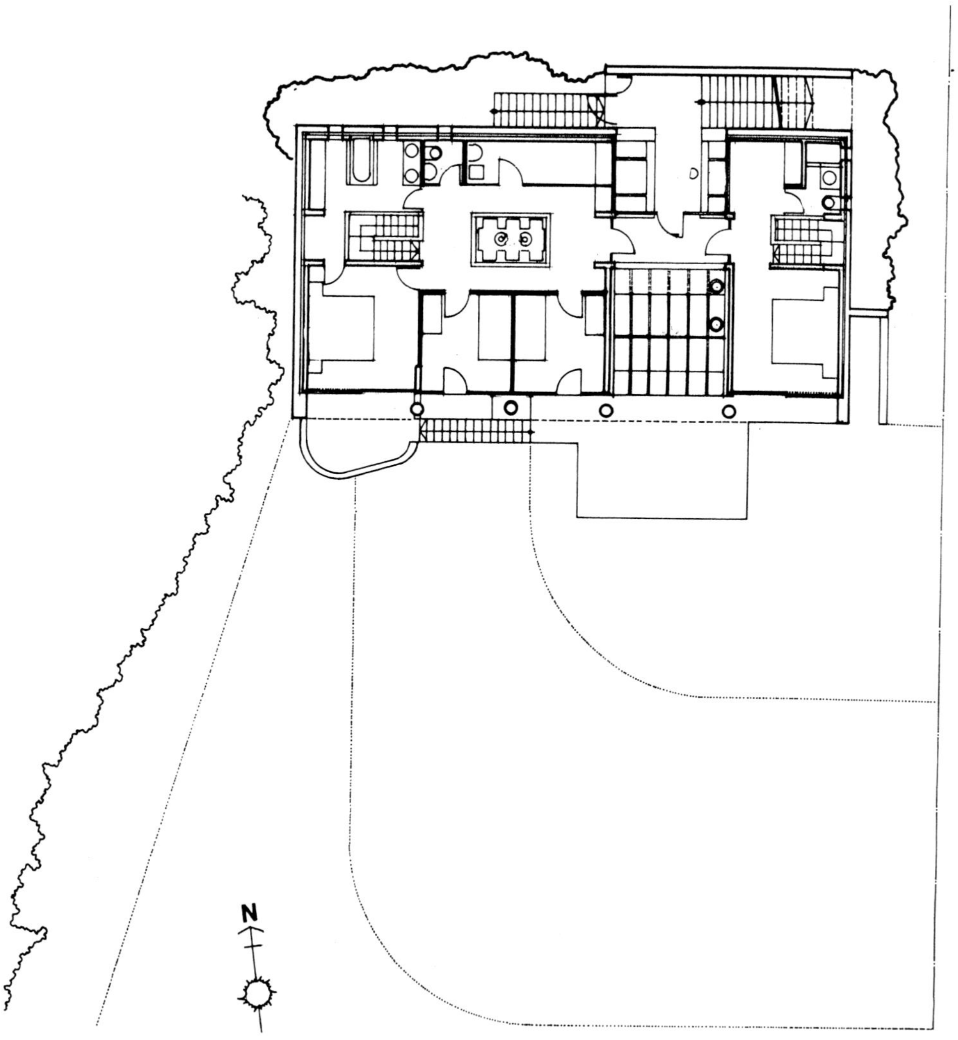

Plan of the upper floor.

that in architecture it takes a long time to impose new energy designs and futuristic expression.

The entrance to the house, below street level and completely covered by glass, is flanked by two larger glass constructions. The fact that the building is mostly glass can best be appreciated from the garden. The winter garden is not only an additional thermal receptor but also forms the link between the house and guest area. It can be reached from the back or the front of the house. The glass roof provides light for the kitchen which is built on a lower level. One noticeable feature at the front is the exquisite red staircase that leads to the bedroom floor from the garden, becoming a balcony at the top, an ideal vantage point overlooking the superb surrounding countryside.

The skylight illuminates the upper floor, mainly devoted to bedroom space.

The upper-floor landing; the use of steel and concrete is evident inside as well as out.

The decoration is mainly in neutral colours, but highlighted with primary shades of red and blue.

The back of the house contains the energy centre on the top floor and the collectors in the glass plaques set at an angle. The entrance to the house is in the middle of the lower level, sheltered by a very striking metal construction.

The house is built on the very top of Bigorio Hill. The panoramic view can be enjoyed from all parts of the house thanks to the glass used in the construction and the south/southwest orientation of each room. The living area, which is in the middle of the building, receives light all day long through the sloping glass panels of the rear part of the collector wall. The installations are all at the back of the house.

The main entrance leads straight into the winter garden, used practically all year round, which furthermore

The spacious winter garden constitutes a lush, sun-bathed morning room.

contains an open hearth. The heat from the fire is of course recycled, and the concrete roof and ceramic floor tiles store any solar heat.

The kitchen is situated behind the winter garden and gives onto the living/dining room. The back wall is white-painted brick and the floor tiles are ceramic. Much is made of the light that comes from the top floor. The living-dining room contains very little furniture, a ceramic-tiled floor and a marvellous view from the windows. The fireplace, made out of concrete with a metal chimney, juts out from the front glass panelling. Around it are designer arm chairs upholstered with natural coloured canvas. The dining room table is in the middle, beneath a skylight which sheds light onto it. The bedrooms upstairs are also lit by the same skylight. This area has been designed with blue metal structures. The master bedroom has a similar interior design to the corridors and the large ceramic tiled terrace which overlooks Sala Capriasca.

In the design for Bigorio House Martin Wagner introduced an innovative and futuristic concept into architecture. A combination of new, efficient passive and active heating techniques in perfect harmony with the natural surroundings, housed in what amounts to a sculpture of glass, steel and concrete, enhanced by the blue and red touches of the windows and railings and the dazzling light of the sky. All this is combined with a marvellous interior, modern and futuristic yet in touch with nature through the clever handing of light and space via the connecting passages, the skylight that extends to

the ground floor, the glass panelling and the interior garden, which integrates the inside with the country outside. Today, this house stands as an example of modern energy design and is greatly admired for its concept and design, as well as being a constant theme of discussion for its technical innovations.

General view over the living room; in the foreground, the dining table, illuminated with either natural or artificial overhead light.

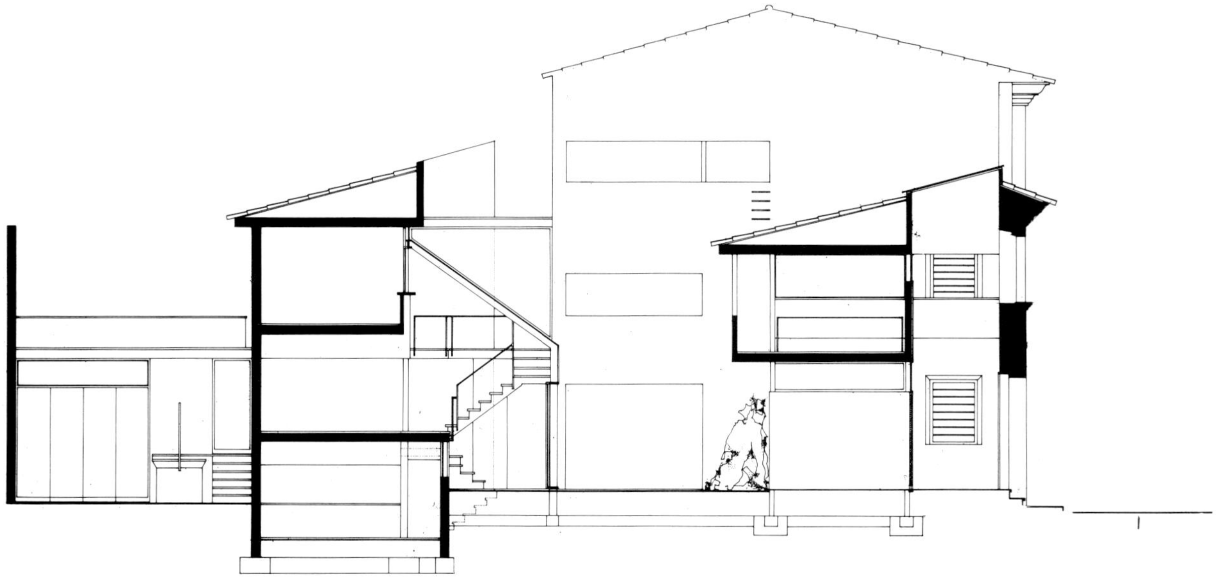

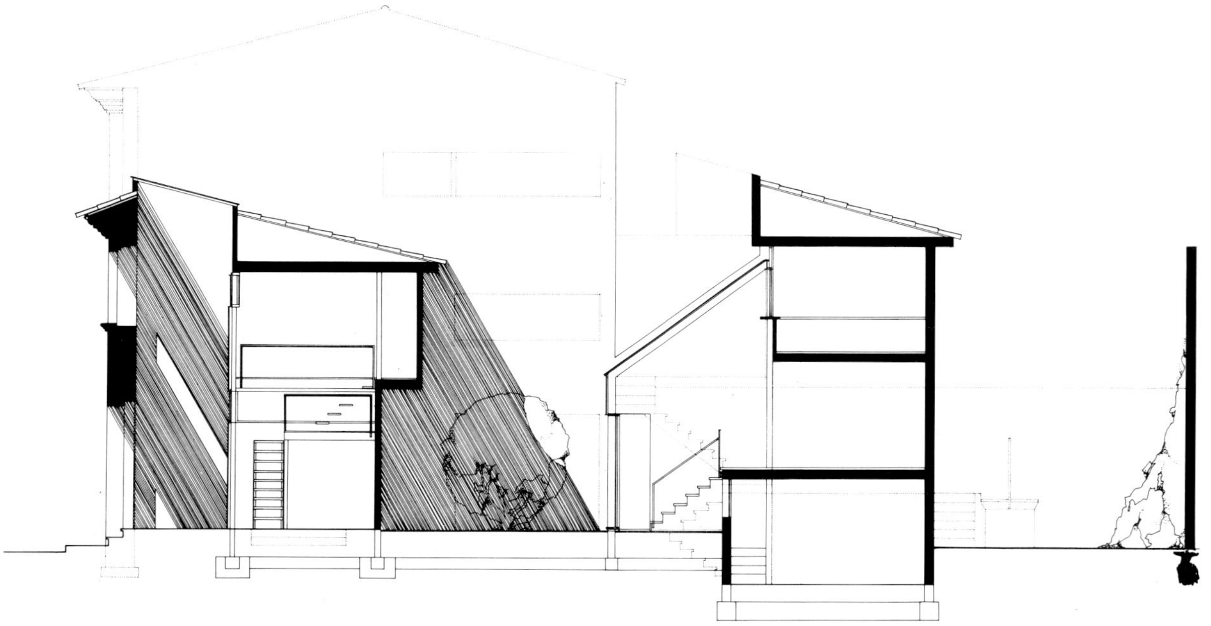

Cross sections of the house.

Sa Pobla House

Miguel Pomar

Miguel Pomar, born in Sa Pobla, graduated from ETSAB (Barcelona Higher Technical School of Architecture) in 1977. During 1978 he served as co-director of the COACB historical archive in the Balearic Islands division. Most of his work was done in Sa Pobla and the surrounding district in the fields of residential architecture and restoration. He first entered for a competition in 1988 and took second prize for his preliminary project for the Ibiza/Formentera secondary school centre. Later he worked with Pere Soler restoring houses in the old quarter of Palma de Mallorca. The projects had been awarded in a competition sponsored by the municipal government.

The project of restoring and converting an old building in Sa Pobla (Majorca) confronted Miguel Pomar once again with the conflict between tradition and modernity and this opposition played a leading role in the scheme. The outcome was a merging of the historical spirit with the new formal organisation imposed by its contemporary function. Furthermore, his desire to make the most of the natural brightness of the Mediterranean environment involved the integration of the process in an indigenous style that posed certain economic and construction problems, which he solved through modern technology.

The original building probably dates from the XVIII century and its main elevation had fronted two adjoining houses in the Calle de la Escuela. The interior space had been distorted by subsequent partitions that resulted in the disunity and lack of coherence of its elements. The residence included a group of outbuildings for farm

The staircase climbs from the photographic studio past the living room, with views into the central courtyard.

Plan of the upper level.

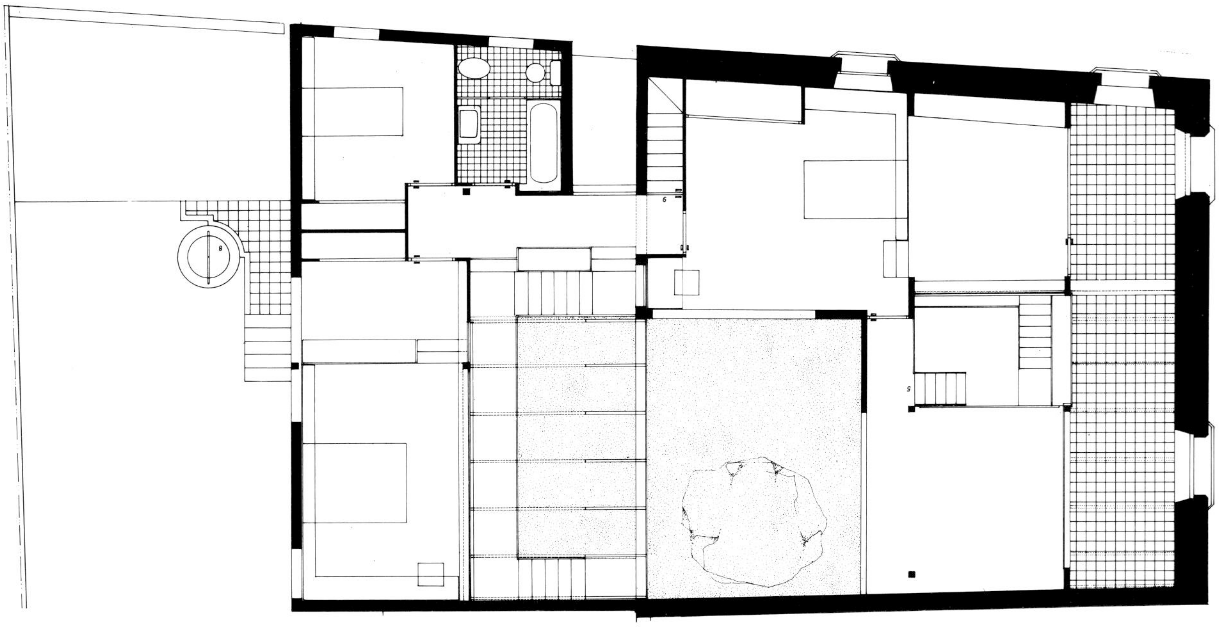

implements and storage that faced the Calle de la Montaña and formed the vertex of that block.

The local administration wanted to preserve the building by means of a conversion that would leave its historical identity intact. But conflicts arose regarding internal structures which did not fulfil new spatial needs, the overall lack of aesthetic and architectural value and the serious deterioration of the abandoned structure.

With all these drawbacks restoration was not feasible, since such a process would not satisfy the demands of its new functional programme. The architect decided to preserve only the main facade on the Calle de la Escuela because of its historical references in Sa Pobla and to initiate a dialogue between the languages of the old order and current trends. Thus the rest of the exterior was disconnected from any previous significance and situated on another, almost timeless plane, in which its external appearance now serves to reflect its new purpose.

The new programme called for the creation of a conventional residence with a photographic studio and a shop selling basic photographic supplies. The internal structural distortion of the original building meant that it had to be completely gutted in order to restructure the physical space and adapt it to the new formal demands.

In short, this project is a fresh conception, not a simple conversion task, and entails a new treatment of dimensions and planes. The purpose of the intervention is not merely formal, but represents an attempt to accommodate the new functional categories. The unoccupied spaces in the interior are used to establish

The sitting room and greenhouse area complement each other, accentuating the use of split levels.

Plan of the lower level.

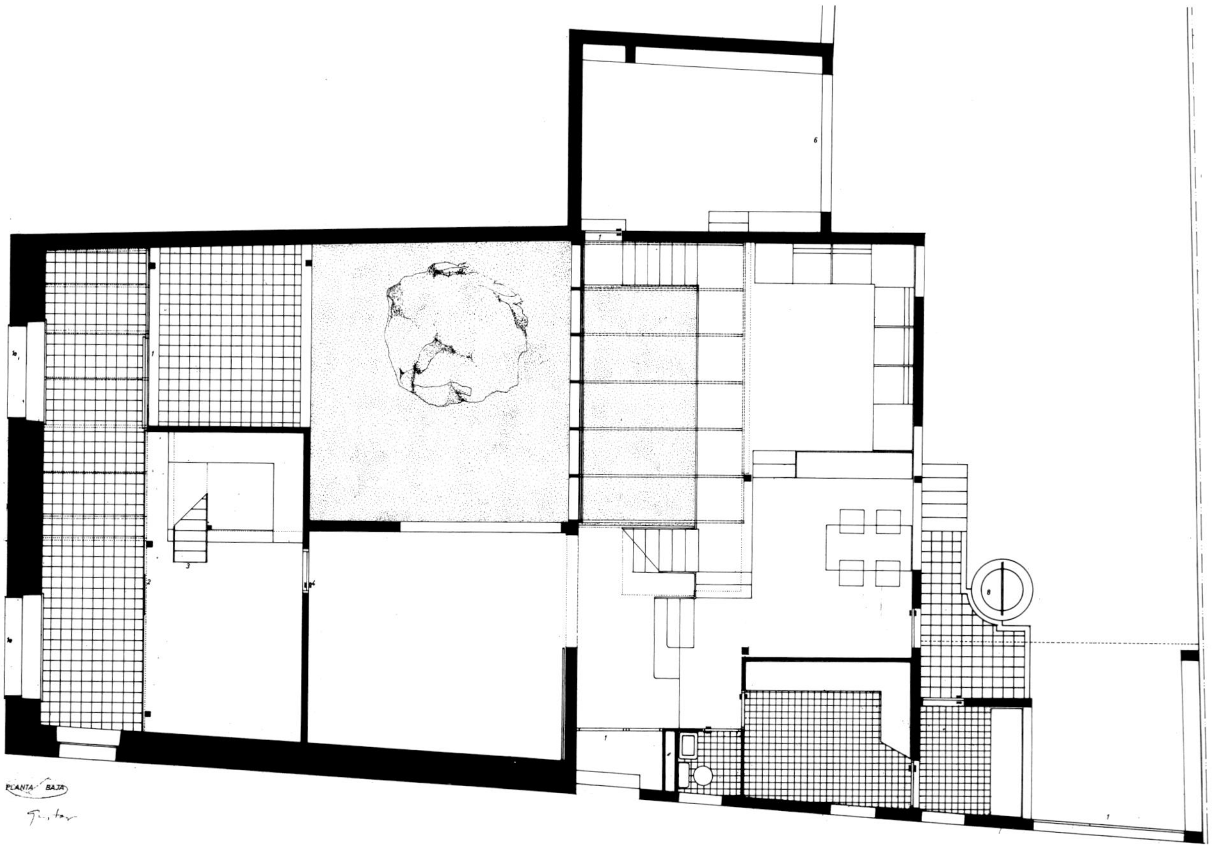

connections between the various rooms and to mark out perspectives for the enrichment of the whole.

The courtyard of the house is especially important in articulating the access to the various sectors. The garden/greenhouse becomes the referential nucleus of the space, visible from all of the rooms that open onto it and are defined by their relation to the courtyard.

The internal architecture is articulated on three floors of differing heights. The basement consists of both domestic and professional areas. The floor above it contains the living room and the dining room and the first floor is given over to bedrooms and provides access to the attic. These three levels are connected by flights of stairs that dominate the residence visually and permit a circulation flow in several directions. The route of the stairway suggests the idea of mobility, which is reinforced by the dissimilarities of the planes, heights and hollows.

The photographic studio in the basement must meet professional and domestic requirements for natural light, and so it is integrated with the courtyard. This means that the living room and the dining room are on different floors and this staggering of levels spills over into the first-floor bedrooms. This variety of heights prevents disproportion in the triple space of the glazed roof and in the photographic studio, as well as in the window sills of the original facade.

The preservation of that facade provoked a conflict that restricted the new formal uses of the structure. The old wall serves no function in the project. It was preserved for purely historical reasons although it

General view of the different levels of the staircase, living room and greenhouse area.

One of the bedrooms, simply furnished and also centred on the axis of the courtyard.

View of the courtyard from the side opposite the living room and greenhouse.

Natural overhead light is one of the great assets of the design.

Differences in ground level are to be found throughout the house.

This view shows how the living room (from which the photo is taken) and the dining room (on the left) are also on different levels.

View down the stairs into the living room, showing the importance of the courtyard as a source of light.

The dining room in the foreground and the living room in the background.

contributes nothing to the essence of the new structure. It is merely a visual element and is not integrated into the functional programme.

Pomar's solution was to build a new glazed facade, set farther back than the original. Thus a type of entrance hall was created, forming the inner courtyard. This new wall forms one side of the photography shop, the entrance to the residence being through sliding screens, and vertically it provides the photography studio with a source of natural light. The studio communicates with a bedroom, offering an unmistakable sexual connotation. The network of relationships between the rooms refers to a series of metaphors whose significance is implicit.

A conventional studio connected to the shop opens onto the courtyard, resulting in a play of visual perspectives from the exterior inwards and vice versa. In addition, the opening of the glazed entrance hall of the residence offers new focal points. The greenhouse becomes a key elements as the central focus of all these perspectives and as the nucleus where all of the spaces of the building converge.

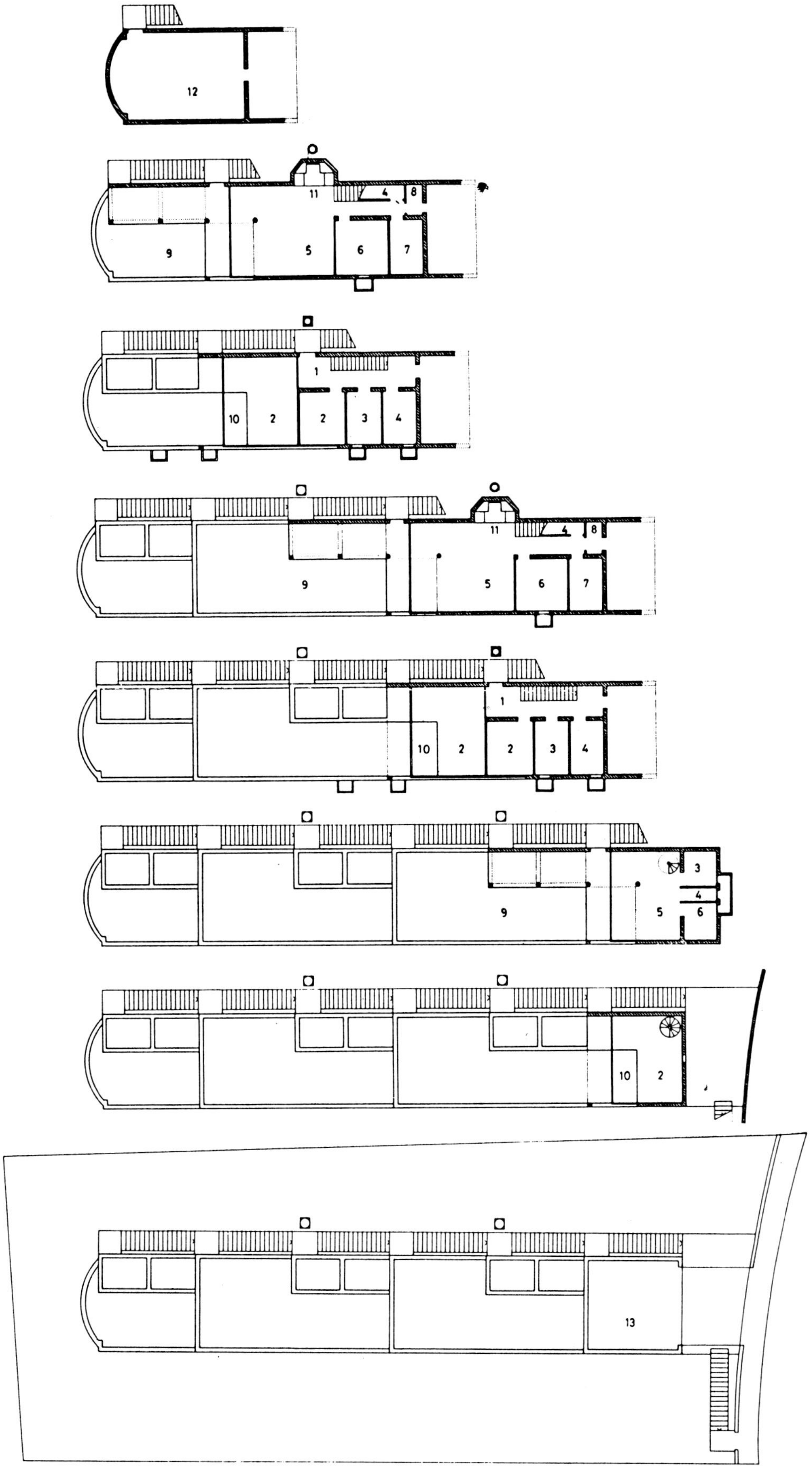
12
11
4
8
9
5
6
7
1
10
2
2
3
4
11
4
8
9
5
6
7
1
10
2
2
3
4
3
4
9
5
6
10
2
13

Floor plans of the various different levels of the three dwellings.

Houses in Montagnola

Mario Campi & Franco Pessina

Born in 1936 in Zurich, Mario Campi trained in the architecture department of the Swiss Federal Institute of Technology in his native city, graduating in 1960. From 1960 to 1961 he worked for the Peppo Brivio Studio in Lugano and in 1962 he went into partnership with Franco Pessina. Campi has been affiliated to the Ticino Order of Engineers and Architects, Swiss Engineers and Architects and the Swiss Federation of Architects. He has taught in prominent American universities. He has been a tenured lecturer at Zurich Polytechnic since 1985 and Rector there since 1988.

Franco Pessina, born in 1933 in Lugano, worked in design and construction, both alone and in association with architectural studios from 1953 to 1961, and in 1962 he joined Mario Campi. He has been a member of REG (Swiss Register of Engineers and Architects) and OTIA since 1974. Four years later he joined SIA and FAS, of which he was elected President in 1990. Since 1985 he has been Professor of Design at the Higher Technical School of Ticino canton in Lugano. Of their joint projects, the most noteworthy have been the 1973 Milan Triennale *and the exhibitions in Zurich, Basel, New York, Boston, Louisville and Montreal.*

The residence built by the Swiss architects Mario Campi and Franco Pessina on the slope of Montagnola Hill reaffirms the expressive coherence of this partnership. The simplicity of the plan, so close to the precepts of Mediterranean structural rationalism, is based on a precise reading of the spatial characteristics, the most economical use of the topographical formation and

The living space is distributed around the well-lit central stairwell.

The decor is conceived with simple, modern lines in a stark aesthetic.

Elevation of the complex.

a volumetric design that initiates an interesting dialogue between the architecture and its excellent position in the surrounding countryside. The two have created a structure that is distinguished by its geometric precision, expressive power and unifying concept.

These three terraced units are situated on a steep slope of Montagnola Hill in the city of Lugano. The architectural setting, dominated by conventional houses, serves to establish a plastic contrast among the various building styles. The site is rather inconvenient due to its long, narrow shape and abrupt incline. The terrain is developed from west to east, starting from the highest contour elevation, at the level of Via Matorell. This exceptional position affords magnificent views of the valley, the city and the splendid lake to the west.

In this difficult but imposing setting, the architects decided on one block moulded with extreme naturalness to the topographical contours, the levels descending the entire length of the slope and adopting a progressive modular design.

The project thus consisted of the linear development of a unified mass, descending from west to east. From the outside the complex seems to be one unit, but its regular, simple geometry forms three articulated components in which the same visual scheme is reproduced. Apart from simplicity and transparency, Campi and Pessina's language is generally based on the fact that, with an expressive economy of means, they succeed in creating a network of extremely complex interconnections.

Both levels take full advantage of the glazed frontage for its view and the natural light it provides.

Section of the complex.

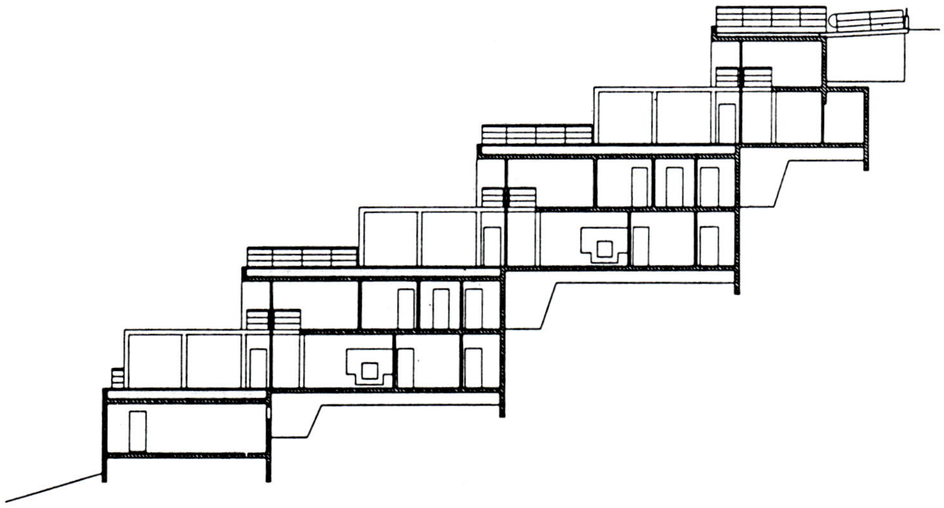

One of the terraces overlooking the lake; the wall is entirely glazed.

From this standpoint, the architects' style is rather distant from the expressionist rationalism of Le Corbusier and closer to the indigenous Mediterranean movement exemplified in Italy by the Figini and Pollini School, by Libera and particularly by Giuseppe Terragni. Their affinity is evidenced by the geometrical precision and structural logic that dominate the building.

The Montagnola houses reflect these rationalist principles in the strategic articulation of the masses, in the highly coherent geometric progression and in the impressive brightness and luminosity of the interior. The volume cascades downward from the highest level, at the Via Matorell, and its external appearance is determined by the various ways in which this extreme difference in levels is handled. The flight of steps that provides access to the three units is built against the south facade. Its aspect is more closed and compact, revealing the levels of the six surfaces, which are interpreted in the interior as duplexes and double heights. There is a door to each unit on every other level. The opposite elevation is more open and does not conceal the slope of the hill, calling attention to the adaptation of the structure to the terrain. The basic geometry of the building is articulated on the northern slope in the three volumes of the housing units.

From a frontal perspective, the complex also reflects the themes of progression and symmetry. Rising from the lowest curved surface, the construction ascends the slope, with a terrace and a glazed facade that occurs three times. The result is an interplay of the static and the dynamic, the opaque and the transparent, exposed

The arrangement of the bedroom is conditioned by the view and the connection with the living room downstairs.

concrete and glazing. The forms are pure and rigid, while in contrast the overall complex appears free-flowing and mobile, owing to the themes introduced in its layout: depth, luminosity and hierarchy.

On this point Campi and Pessina have sucessfully integrated the complex visual relationships in the residence by means of basic and elementary forms. Firstly, the pergolas on the west face provide tension and at the same time a certain visual ordering. These structures are formed at the meeting of the extension of the west facade and the small balcony on the first level of each module. The partitions that protect the privacy of these terrace areas are reflected in the formal difference between each of the lateral facades. This distinction is reinforced by the precise placement of openings in the elevations, which affects the visual rhythm of the composition.

To distribute the programme, the architects designed an interior layout in which the more significant rooms communicate with the best views of the setting, insofar as this was possible. In pursuit of this goal, Campi and Pessina focused on the motifs of space and light, ordering the different rooms according to the scenery. The three modules were laid out in the same way, although the highest of them is smaller.

The two end components contain communal facilities; the top level is a parking area while the cellar on the bottom level is curvilinear. Each volume has two floors and an entrance on the south flank that is reached by the descending flight of steps built against that wall. The

The dining area connects visually and functionally with the kitchen by means of a large hatch.

complex has a total of seven horizontal planes, which have a greater vertical development on the living-room levels, achieved through an opening in the slab that separates the floors, thus creating the double height. The more important rooms are in this area, communicating with the exterior through continuous glazing that begins on the northern front. In addition to the entrance halls and the vast living rooms, the ground floor also houses the kitchen and other facilities. These latter spaces are partially underground because of the gradient of the land. The fireplaces are on the south, penetrating the terrain, and the flues emerge from the ground at a point beyond the lateral flight of steps, creating a striking visual effect.

On the second level, the rooms overlooking the valley open onto small balconies whose supporting structures in reinforced cement are extended to form the pergolas that frame the visual sequences from the interior rooms. To make the most of the available space, the roof of each module serves as the terrace for the one above it, one of the most effective strategies of the complex. Their light metal railings and the grass growing on the outer section create a visual transition to the greenery of the landscape.

Mario Campi and Franco Pessina's design for this small residential building is based on the precepts of Mediterranean rationalism. Using a pure, limited geometric vocabulary, they succeed in establishing a highly complex network of relationships. The components take on a dynamic and free-flowing appearance, elegantly expressing the construction process with its interior programme.

Houses in Montagnola

The dining area connects visually and functionally with the kitchen by means of a arge hatch.

complex has a total of seven horizontal planes, which have a greater vertical development on the living-room levels, achieved through an opening in the slab that separates the floors, thus creating the double height. The more important rooms are in this area, communicating with the exterior through continuous glazing that begins on the northern front. In addition to the entrance halls and the vast living rooms, the ground floor also houses the kitchen and other facilities. These latter spaces are partially underground because of the gradient of the land. The fireplaces are on the south, penetrating the terrain, and the flues emerge from the ground at a point beyond the lateral flight of steps, creating a striking visual effect.

On the second level, the rooms overlooking the valley open onto small balconies whose supporting structures in reinforced cement are extended to form the pergolas that frame the visual sequences from the interior rooms. To make the most of the available space, the roof of each module serves as the terrace for the one above it, one of the most effective strategies of the complex. Their light metal railings and the grass growing on the outer section create a visual transition to the greenery of the landscape.

Mario Campi and Franco Pessina's design for this small residential building is based on the precepts of Mediterranean rationalism. Using a pure, limited geometric vocabulary, they succeed in establishing a highly complex network of relationships. The components take on a dynamic and free-flowing appearance, elegantly expressing the construction process with its interior programme.